Questions

# The Hindu Sound

**Questions**

A series of explorations by
William Corlett & John Moore

THE QUESTION OF RELIGION
THE CHRIST STORY
THE HINDU SOUND

*in preparation*

THE JUDAIC LAW
THE BUDDHA WAY
THE ISLAMIC SPACE

WILLIAM CORLETT
&
JOHN MOORE

# The Hindu Sound

HAMISH HAMILTON
LONDON

First published in Great Britain 1978 by
Hamish Hamilton Ltd., 90 Great Russell Street,
London WC1B 3PT

ISBN 0 241 89772 6

Printed in Great Britain by
Ebenezer Baylis and Son Ltd.
The Trinity Press, Worcester, and London

This book is one of a series.

The titles are *The Question of Religion*, *The Christ Story*, *The Hindu Sound*, *The Judaic Law*, *The Buddha Way* and *The Islamic Space*. The books were written in the order as listed, but this in no way implies any suggested precedence of one religion over another, nor any preference on the part of the authors. Each book may be read in its own right, rather as each note of an octave may sound alone.

However, for an octave to be complete, it depends on the developing frequency and character of each note. In the same way, it has been the experience of the authors, approaching this series as one work, to find a similar development as they progressed from one book to another.

*That is perfect. This is perfect. Perfect comes from perfect. Take*
*perfect from perfect, the remainder is perfect.*

*May peace and peace and peace be everywhere.*

*Whatever lives is full of the Lord. Claim nothing; enjoy, do not*
*covet His property.*

*Then hope for a hundred years of life doing your duty. No other*
*way can prevent deeds from clinging, proud as you are of your human*
*life.*

*They that deny the Self, return after death to a godless birth, blind,*
*enveloped in darkness.*

*The Self is one. Unmoving, it moves faster than the mind. The senses*
*lag, but Self runs ahead. Unmoving, it outruns pursuit. Out of Self*
*comes the breath that is the life of all things.*

*Unmoving, it moves; is far away, yet near; within all, outside all.*

*Of a certainty the man who can see all creatures in himself, himself*
*in all creatures, knows no sorrow.*

*How can a wise man, knowing the unity of life, seeing all creatures in*
*himself, be deluded or sorrowful?*

*The Self is everywhere, without a body, without a shape, whole,*
*pure, wise, all knowing, far shining, self-depending, all transcending;*
*in the eternal procession assigning to every period its proper duty.*

*Pin your faith to natural knowledge, stumble through the darkness*
*of the blind; pin your faith to supernatural knowledge, stumble through*
*a darkness deeper still.*

*Natural knowledge brings one result, supernatural knowledge another.*
*We have heard it from the wise who have clearly explained it.*

*They that know and can distinguish between natural knowledge and*
*supernatural knowledge shall, by the first, cross the perishable in safety;*
*shall, passing beyond the second, attain immortal life.*

*Pin your faith to the seed of nature, stumble through the darkness of* the blind; pin your faith to the shapes of nature, stumble through a darkness deeper still.

The seed of nature brings one result; the shapes of nature another. We have heard it from the wise, who have clearly explained it.

They that know and can distinguish between the shapes of nature and the seed of nature shall, by the first, cross the perishable in safety; shall, passing beyond the second, attain immortal life.

They have put a golden stopper into the neck of the bottle. Pull it, Lord! Let out reality. I am full of longing.

Protector, Seer, controller of all, fountain of life, upholder, do not waste light; gather light; let me see that blessed body—Lord of all. I myself am He.

Life merge into the all prevalent, the eternal; body turn to ashes. Mind! meditate on the eternal Spirit; remember past deeds. Mind! remember past deeds; remember, Mind! remember.

Holy Light! illuminate the way that we may gather the good we planted. Are not our deeds known to you? Do not let us grow crooked, we that kneel and pray again and again.

*Eesha-Upanishad*

# The Hindu Sound

If I open a book and read words written along a line, followed by another line and after that another . . . What happens?

Do the words convey a meaning to me?

Why are they there?

Do I want to know who wrote them?

Were they written by someone in order that he could speak to me?

I am now writing words upon a page and you are reading them.

Why am I writing them? Why are you reading them?

Are we not both expressing a need? I to be understood and you to understand?

But:

How can there be anything that I have to say that you do not already know?

Where did I acquire knowledge that you do not possess? From someone else? Then, where did that other person acquire the knowledge? From someone else?

And you, having read the book—will you have any more knowledge than you have now? How can that possibly be? All that you will have done will be to have read a string of words along a line, followed by another line, and after that another.

Indeed, the process has already begun.

I, the writer, have started stringing words along a line; you, the reader, have looked at them, one by one, and you are responding to them.

But where am I getting the words from, and where the ideas that the words are attempting to express?

Over the centuries, man has come to rely upon the written word to express ideas and concepts.

We write letters to each other when we are not together; we leave notes for each other. We put down on paper what we would have said to each other if we had been face to face.

But the word on the page and the spoken word have one vast difference.

*A word is a sound.*

The way the word is spoken, the *emotion* in the voice of the speaker, can radically change its meaning.

"I hate you" can be spoken playfully—and can sound full of love.

To express such a complicated game on the page would require a paragraph of explanatory notes.

\*

We are about to embark upon a journey into the labyrinth of the mind, pursuing *The Question of Religion,* through the ancient scriptures of India—the doctrines and the wisdom of the Vedas.

We will be using as our source material ancient writings, first set down in Sanskrit. In particular we will be drawing upon the *Bhagavad-Gita* (called "The Song of God") and the principal *Upanishads* (a word meaning literally "At the feet of").

Who wrote these works and who spoke these words we may discover, or we may find that the author in unimportant. For the essence of the *Gita* is the word SONG.

If you can read music, then you could sit down and read through a musical score; but obviously for the score to be music, it must be made SOUND.

I wonder what it is in us that responds to a musical sound?

Why can sounds—musical sounds—stir the emotions? We can be "moved" by music, we can be "uplifted" by music, we even sometimes say that we are "transported" by music.

What is going on?

What IS music?

First and foremost—it is SOUND.

And sound seems to connect with our emotions.

Thus, one doesn't usually say that one *understands* music so much as that one *feels* it.

It is an affair of the heart.

\*

*Mind! remember past deeds; remember, Mind! remember.*

*

When we "remember"—what happens?

Do we actually re-live the past moment?

Or—do we for a moment *feel* as we felt then?

A waft of scent can send us winging back to our earliest childhood, a phrase of music can evoke an eternal longing . . . for what?

We will never really be able to express in words how our deepest emotions are experienced; we will resort to meaningless *clichés*.

We will say something like:

"My heart stirred . . ."

*

*The Hindu Sound* must be an exploration as much for the writers as it is for the reader; for it is to do with the inexpressible.

*The Hindu Sound* is in the HEART.

*

*In this body, in this town of Spirit, there is a little house shaped like a lotus, and in that house there is a little space. One should know what is there.*

*What is there? Why is it so important?*

*There is as much in that space within the heart, as there is in the whole world outside.*

*Heaven, earth, fire, wind, sun, moon, lightning, stars; whatever is and whatever is not, everything is there.*

*(Chhandogya-Upanishad)*

*

So, what have these sacred songs to do with me?

Why should a series of ancient doctrines from Asia have any possible bearing upon my present situation?

There may be wisdom there—but is it a wisdom that can speak to me?

Have we, the writers—and you, the readers—anything in common?

I was born into this world; you were born into this world.

Did we choose to be here?

My mind, with its concept of what it has learned to call "choice", thinks not: how could I possibly choose to be conceived?

My mind thinks it is I who am sitting here and that I "began" a certain number of years ago when a human ovum was fertilized. Therefore it is a logical impossibility . . . how could I choose to originate myself?

So; if I did not choose to be here—then, therefore, I did not choose my parents, nor where I was born, nor when.

Ordinarily my mind cannot comprehend any other explanation and so it takes the above as undeniable fact and does not think about it very much—if at all.

I may occasionally pause to wonder how this person called "me" came to be blessed with certain good fortune or cursed by certain ill fortune, but as there seems no logical answer to that either, I simply have to "thank my lucky stars" or "bemoan my lot", as the case may be.

In fact, the more I come to consider it, I seem to have to take a lot for granted about the circumstances of my existence; and, since so much of it does not appear to have a logical explanation, I have to withdraw from such problems and admit lamely: "It just happened that way."

*

*Whatever lives is full of the Lord. Claim nothing; enjoy, do not covet His property.*

*

Then I grew up; as you grew up.

Born without choice, we experience an environment and influences that were also not of our choosing. How could we have chosen the homes in which we spent our childhood, or the society in which we found ourselves?

What I learned of the world in my childhood was taught to me by my parents and guardians, my relations and teachers, my friends and acquaintances—or from books, radio, television and so forth. My mind has to admit that my experience was utterly arbitrary, haphazard, accidental. I did not choose what happened to come my way each day. Even if I decided to do certain things or go to certain places, there was never any choice as to what *actually happened* in the event.

Perhaps I had some choice in what I learned in the sense that I was interested in some things and not in others, that I accepted some things and rejected others. But did I do this consciously and with good reason?

Do I have any *choice* in what I like and what I dislike?

Do I have any choice in what I now "choose" to accept and what I now "choose" to reject?

It all depends upon what I think of as "choice".

Now I may not have choice in what happens to me—but, perhaps, I *do* have choice in how I deal with it *when it is actually happening*.

However, further back still, did I have any choice in the sort of mind that I have and how it works? Did I choose to have the criteria through which I now find myself liking and disliking, desiring or fearing?

In other words . . . how did I come by my particular disposition of mind—attracted to some things and repulsed by others? Did I *choose* to have the particular inclinations by which I judge?

The further back—or deeper—that I question what I have assumed was the freedom to choose, the more I begin to wonder if in fact I have ever had any choice at all!

\*

*Then hope for a hundred years of life doing your duty. No other way can prevent deeds from clinging, proud as you are of your human life.*

\*

And so I matured; as you matured.

We each became "somebody" in our own estimation and right.

It may be enough to go on from there and simply to live out the rest of our lives, just being "somebody"—possibly a special "somebody", each to himself—but probably just an ordinary "somebody" as far as the world is concerned, especially if it has not had the benefit of knowing us.

But what do *I* know about this "somebody", with whom I live every day of my life, and whom I call "me"?

How did this "me" come to be?

I look into my mind and I see that somehow, gradually, everything acquired through the years of my existence constitutes what I think of as "me". And, because the collection of characteristics, qualities and possessions provided since my conception is peculiar to this individual being, then, not only do I think of it as "me" but, because everyone else recognizes its uniqueness, they think of it as "me" as well. And because of your collective peculiarities, I will be able to identify you also.

It doesn't really matter how this collection came about—the ideas, beliefs, assumptions, attitudes, opinions and acquired learning are mine. And I believe, not unnaturally, that they are what make "me" what I am.

BUT, if all these characteristics and attributes were acquired, whether apparently through choice or not, and if they are therefore my "possessions", to whom do they belong?

Me?

Can I be both the sum total of what has been acquired AND that which acquired them?

Which is me?

*Who am I?*

What is the essential, and originally innocent, central core of this being—the "is-ness" of being here—upon which all these acquisitions have been impressed or superimposed?

Who was I before I became conscious of being "me"?

*

*They that deny the Self, return after death to a godless birth, blind, enveloped in darkness.*

*The Self is one. Unmoving, it moves faster than the mind. The senses lag, but Self runs ahead. Unmoving, it outruns pursuit. Out of Self comes the breath that is the life of all things.*

*Unmoving, it moves; is far away, yet near; within all, outside all.*

*

Eventually, I will die; as you will die.

This is something that the mind dislikes thinking about—perhaps, again, because it tends to take the attitude that death is a problem that can either be left until later or is best ignored because it is beyond the scope of mind to solve.

"Eventually," thinking mind may say, "it is all going to end. But for now, I will get on with living . . ."

For, if the mind has adopted the belief that all the attributes and acquisitions constitute "me", then it seems evident that, at death, they will all disperse or be destroyed—and that therefore "me" will go with them.

But—what about that "essential core of being"?

What happens to that at death?

Mind is baffled. If it does not comprehend where the being "came from" in the first place, it is hardly likely to understand where it "goes to".

So, the mind tends to adjust itself to what it can cope with, according to its learning. It dismisses, or vaguely compensates for, what appears to be outside its comprehension—where "me" came from at birth at the one extreme and where "me" goes to at death at the other. It confines itself instead to concern for living the part in between. It settles for the finite, the phenomenal world of things, the *learning* necessary for getting by from day to day in the most enjoyable and comfortable manner devisable, "choosing" the pleasant in preference to the painful.

And why shouldn't it? Why should mind worry—even if it had time—about the infinite, the "unknown", the "beyond", the first causes, the whys and wherefores, that will not fit into logical and scientific structures?

It is as if mind creates a "bubble" for itself, a sort of cocoon, which is a sphere of conditional learning, within which it is concerned to construct "models" which will serve as the basis for behaviour, and with which it can deal, hopefully, with any demands made on it by the happenings of the world.

Within this sphere (with all its habitual processes, used time and time again) mind can occupy itself, amuse itself, frighten itself, dream about things, think to itself, talk to itself. It creates a private world, which is able to accommodate new events and absorb them into its structures and is also able to resist unwelcome invasions.

It may, simply, choose not to think about something—because it upsets the *status quo*!

Providing the security of this inner world can be maintained intact, then life in the world outside can be most entertaining, interesting and enjoyable.

But the trouble is that this "island" is all too often threatened and disturbed.

*

*Of a certainty the man who can see all creatures in himself, himself in all creatures, knows no sorrow.*

*How can a wise man, knowing the unity of life, seeing all creatures in himself, be deluded or sorrowful?*

*The Self is everywhere, without a body, without a shape, whole, pure, wise, all knowing, far shining, self-depending, all transcending; in the eternal procession assigning to every period its proper duty.*

*

Mind, however, would separate itself off.

Mind believes itself to be separate from all other minds.

Mind suggests that all things are separate.

Mind considers itself the separate centre, an island, in a sea of separate creatures, of separate things.

*

So, does the wisdom of the world offer any alternative?

Yes, it does.

But before we explore what the alternative may be—in this case through Hindu wisdom—let us establish a platform from which to venture into this strange and wonderful conundrum.

*

What do I mean by wisdom; and what do you mean by wisdom?
Do we already have it?
Is it acquired?
Or, does it "grow"?
In order to become wise, is it a case of learning as much as possible?
Or is it a case of an innate sense or knowledge—that perhaps has to be invoked and developed?
We could no doubt use the space of a whole book on this subject alone—but we cannot do that, so let us make one or two simple propositions.
Firstly, a vast accumulation of learned facts does not guarantee wisdom. We could say that it is evident in human history that the acknowledged "wise men" of the past have not necessarily been "educated" in the sense that we usually understand "education".
Secondly—and this is one reason for the first proposition—wisdom is essentially connected with the ability to cope with life's problems, and not with intellectual exercises.
We could therefore deduce that wisdom has to do with understanding, experience and an ability to learn from—and hence to cope with—what happens to us in life.
Further, we could surmise that wisdom is a knowledge that everyone has in potential and that it "grows" according to the ability of the individual to relate it to what he learns and experiences.

*

*Pin your faith to natural knowledge, stumble through the darkness of the blind; pin your faith to supernatural knowledge, stumble through the darkness deeper still.*

*Natural knowledge brings one result; supernatural knowledge another. We have heard it from the wise who have clearly explained it.*

*They that know and can distinguish between natural knowledge and supernatural knowledge shall, by the first, cross the perishable in safety; shall, passing beyond the second, attain immortal life.*

*

How, then, can wisdom be linked with choice?

Obviously in the wordly sense, we appear to have a "choice". I may "choose" to do something or not to do something, or acquire one thing in preference to another. However, such choices could be the result of previous conditioning and hence it could be claimed that they are not "pure" choice.

Again, there would be enough potential discussion here to fill another book—and, yet again, we must be content with one or two simple propositions.

Ultimately, we can say, we have *no choice* in the fact that we are endowed with *the capacity to choose*! If we decide that there is no such thing as "choice"—we have already chosen!

But it is a strange phenomenon, if we look into it seriously—for what we have to admit is that we have *no choice* in what we are given or presented with to choose from or among!

Given that I have no choice in what happens to me at any given moment, I exercise choice in all manner of ways as a result of the experience—and this, as we have suggested earlier, is conditioned by what beliefs, attitudes, ideas, etc. I have acquired by accident.

So what gives "me" the sense that choice is real and immediate?

Perhaps it is that I have the sense—each time I am conscious of a choice before me—that if I am to avoid making a wrong choice I must bring to bear what wisdom I can.

For what is *not* conditioned, in this sense, is the degree to which I can make a *wiser* choice.

And, paradoxically, perhaps, we may discover that wisdom is not so much to do with acquiring new beliefs and attitudes but discarding, disbelieving, dispensing with all that I have acquired unconsciously and in ignorance.

In other words—*wisdom* may be seen to have something to do with *choosing consciously* to free the mind of its conditioning.

18

It could be argued that all the above is relative and just playing with words—but it is a serious matter.

If you think that you have free choice and that you are as wise as you can be . . . then, fair enough.

But if you do *not*, then the question is inevitably posed:

"Whose choice is it, then . . . that I am here; that I have experience; that I am moved to try to understand what wisdom is and how I may become wiser?"

And, if any of us hold such questions, then you could say that we have no choice but to consider and explore them!

*

*Pin your faith to the seed of nature, stumble through the darkness of the blind; pin your faith to the shapes of nature, stumble through a darkness deeper still.*

*The seed of nature brings one result; the shapes of nature another. We have heard it from the wise, who have clearly explained it.*

*They that know and can distinguish between the shapes of nature and the seed of nature shall, by the first, cross the perishable in safety; shall, passing beyond the second, attain immortal life.*

*

A further plank in our platform from which to explore the "world's wisdom"—and, in this book, the Hindu standpoint in particular—is that there is a recognition of a certain distinction between the accumulation of learning in this world that creates the identity of this particular person—"me" (or the phenomenal ego)—and the inner core of being, the inner sense of existing which gives rise to the experience "I am"—regardless of what I may, since birth, have become.

This is essential because, if there is a commitment to the belief that "me" is what I really am, then there is no choice but to accept that there is only this world's existence and that death is a final and inevitable end.

(There are various assertions and so-called cases of evidence that suggest that "me" does continue after death of the body in some other realm. It is up to the individual, according to his wisdom, to choose whether to believe this or not. However, if we continue to consider "wisdom"—such as that which inspired the Hindu religion —we may be led to a quite other understanding of "life hereafter". At such a time "me" may be seen to be *material* in this life, but *immaterial* in the "hereafter").

\*

*They have put a golden stopper into the neck of the bottle. Pull it, Lord! Let out reality. I am full of longing.*

\*

Wisdom—which at root has connection with two words: "knowledge" and "lord"—is uncompromising; it does not brook the mind's self-delusion.

Sooner or later, he who thinks and acts in ignorance and foolishness has to meet the consequences.

We could say that wisdom has to do with *understanding* (standing under) the reality of our being here in the world and what our responsibilities (our abilities to respond) are whilst we are here.

\*

And now we begin to focus on the subject of this book.

\*

Given the history of mankind and all its endeavour (relatively short-lived in terms of the life of the earth), what has man managed to understand?

What wisdom could be said to have been distilled from the lives of millions upon millions of human beings?

Can we assume that today we are at the peak of human wisdom— however "high" that may be—or that we have much further to go, in however many more thousand years mankind continues?

Can we assume that we are wiser today than ever before, because

20

so much learning has been derived from the relatively sophisticated and informed advances of the Scientific Age?

Or is wisdom some kind of constant which men have always been capable of realizing in their own way—but which seems to advance and recede through the ages according to the number of men at any one time who are realizing it?

Do we have good reason to assume that the further we go back into past history the more ignorant men will have been?

As we look at the state of human relationships around the world today, can we with validity say that we have advanced very much in wisdom and understanding?

Would it be a relief, perhaps a refreshing one, not to have to assume that the ultimate peak of human wisdom is something we will never see in this life?

Might it be that not only has it been realized by man in the past but that it may be realized *now*?

If we look closely, would it be true to say that wisdom is *not* essentially something that can be *learned* from history, from books, from study—in fact, *from anyone else*—but that it is a living experience and manifestation *in the individual* here and now?

How can there be any wisdom "out there"?

We must try and test our experience in order that we may understand what it may be to be wise—each for "*ourself*".

How can *you* be wise for me?

How can I be wise for you?

There has to be a realizing *by us* as to what is ignorant, foolish and illusory *in ourselves* for us to be able to *become* wiser.

*

*Protector, Seer, controller of all, fountain of life, upholder, do not waste light; gather light; let me see that blessed body—Lord of all. I myself am He.*

*

History suggests that through our accumulated learning we have increased our ability to influence the environment by manipulating

21

the resources of the earth—and that, presumably, has a significance in the evolution of the universe that we cannot fully understand.

But you and I—biologically speaking—have a brief span on this planet, at best one hundred years.

We have relatively little time. What are we supposed to do with it? Do we imagine that, in terms of "self-development" we can accomplish any more in that time than did our ancestors? Or do we have exactly the same opportunity as they had in order to attain the same realization (the making *real*) of the meaning of our lives? The "trappings" may be different, and I may have access to far more scientific information, but in essence—in my living with myself and in my potential for understanding the truth and purpose of my existence—do I have any advantage over a Roman emperor, a prehistoric Celt, a tribal Indian, an Elizabethan alchemist, a disciple of Jesus, or of the Buddha . . . ?

Maybe I do; maybe I don't. I do not know.

I can only, if I am moved, decide to assemble my available abilities and capacities and bring them to bear on my present life.

Then, observing my experience, questioning what is happening, learning from my mistakes and taking what advantage I can from the reports and messages of those who have spoken on such matters in the past, I may hope to become "wiser".

\*

*Life merge into the all prevalent, the eternal; body turn to ashes. Mind! meditate on the eternal Spirit; remember past deeds. Mind! remember past deeds; remember, Mind! remember.*

\*

I wonder where and when the first attempt was made to pass on wisdom?

We cannot know the answer because such attempts, presumably by word of mouth—by *sound*—evidently precede recorded history. But among the first evidence—and probably the oldest known surviving evidence—is that collection of scriptures known as the *Vedas*. The word is derived from the Sanskrit "*vid*" which means "to know", and they are thus, essentially, to do with "knowledge".

The Vedas are said to be *"anadi"* which means "without beginning"—and this implies that not only does no one know how far back in time the knowledge goes, nor who first spoke it, but that it has *no beginning*.

Here, immediately, is an implied challenge to the ordinary, logical mind's concept of time and sequence. *No beginning*—how can that be?

Mind has to cease its obsession with past and future and consider the proposition that it may be able to realize another "time", and that certain knowledge is not subject to birth and death, but that it exists "eternally".

*

Knowledge—without beginning; knowledge—without end.

Man will never quite find the "words" to express it.

This is a challenge that mind may well resist!

For, if there are no words to express this unfamiliar concept, then, no doubt, it is too abstract for mind to encompass.

And—if the concept is too abstract for mind, then—intellectually—is it worth bothering about?

"It is all beyond me," my mind may say. (And we may discover that it *is*, precisely, that: it *is beyond "me"*!)

Yes; the concept is abstract;

*Knowledge—without a beginning; knowledge—without an end.*

But that is the nature of all knowledge; it comes from, or out of . . . where?

We say—first the idea, then the idea formulated, then understanding, then realization. It will no longer be "abstract" when mind, reaching for the concept, "touches" it, understands (stands under) and realizes it (makes it real).

But where did the idea come from?

*

This book is called *The Hindu Sound*. What is a sound? Where does it come from? What happens to mind when it listens to music?

Perhaps, if we ever feel like a "break" from this book; when mind is tired and frustrated and irritated by the abstract, we should put it down (the book) and listen to some music. It doesn't matter what music; not at first . . . (And—if you don't like music—listen to birds singing, water flowing) . . . Just listen to sound.

Where is mind?

What is it doing?

Is mind claiming that the sound is "abstract"? That it cannot "understand" it?

No, we may say, mind is resting.

Why should listening to sound rest the mind?

And—much more extraordinary—why should we, suddenly, unexpectedly, be "moved" by sound?

Could we say that it is the peculiar nature of *sound* that it may transcend the logical working of mind and that it may touch the heart?

And, when the heart is pierced, what then may flow?

The *Upanishads* have many tantalizing and mysterious statements to make about the heart. Here is just one, from the *Katha-Upanishad*:

*The heart has a hundred and one arteries; one of these—Sushumna —goes up into the head. He who climbs through it attains immortality; others drive him into the vortex.*

As we listen to sounds—really listen; as we listen to music— music . . . of our "choice"?—then perhaps our taste for "sound" will become refined, defined, fine: perhaps we will seek for "pure" sound, for the origins of sound.

The *Vedas*, the *Upanishads*, the *Bhagavad-Gita* were, before they were written down, spoken—and not just spoken, but sung.

Wisdom contained in song, and song containing sound.

Why do birds "sing"?

Why can the mind rest on a sound?

Why?

What does it mean to say:

*Mind! meditate on the eternal Spirit . . . ?*

24

What does it mean?

Where is mind in meditation?

Where is mind when it is listening?

Listen to some music—really listen: what is mind doing? What is being done to mind?

Meditation is the cornerstone of the Vedic philosophy.

The *Upanishads* are not to be read for their meaning only, but for their *sound*: for what they *do* to mind—not just what they *mean* to mind.

\*

And how mind wants to reject it all!

"What is the point? What purpose can any of it have in relation to my everyday living?"

"What difference will it make? Why should it matter to 'me'?"

\*

*Holy light! illuminate the way that we may gather the good we planted. Are not our deeds known to you? Do not let us grow crooked, we that kneel and pray again and again.*

\*

The "ageless wisdom" which gave rise to the Vedas was also known as *Sanatana Dharma* which could be translated as "Eternal Law" and it is the implication of law which gives the clue—because the essence of useful and purposeful behaviour is that it should be lawful.

This does not mean just obeying the man-made laws of society nor accepting the inescapable laws of nature; it means *realizing* the laws which govern mind—which manifest in what we may call "morality". For, according to our morals—or the lack of them—so we behave more or less responsibly in respect of ourselves and others. (But, here again, be sharp. Mind! Not the habitual moral mores of our society—but the morals inherent within each of us . . . coming from where?)

The word "*dharma*" has a deep and far-reaching meaning. It speaks of an all-embracing code of wisdom which influences all

25

human conduct, especially the individual responsibility and duty to the self, all other fellow humans, and the environment.

And this, of course, embraces what we call the "religious" or "spiritual" aspect of human life.

Religion is not—nor should it be—just bland dogma and repetitive ritual. It is not just a part-time occupation which one can take or leave; it is not, nor could it be, something in addition to all the other activities in life. Religious understanding ought to be the mind's inspiration *at all times*, influencing and directing every decision and action.

No matter where I am, no matter what I may be doing—there can be religion in its truest, purest form. Every time I *really* listen, that is meditation.

It is in relation to this understanding that any meaningful "choice" can be made: for the "choice" can only be the discarding of the untruth in the hope of realizing truth, the dispelling of illusion in order to discover reality.

*

The Hindu Sound, the doctrine and wisdom of the Vedas, has been called the Perennial Philosophy. From before recorded time its song has sounded; its music is with us still.

To listen to it, we must drop so many of our habitual responses of mind. And wouldn't that be a relief? To be able to hear something as if for the first time; fresh and clean, without our usual preconceptions; no longer dragging "me" around.

*Sound, transcending mind—touching the heart.*

As we approach The Hindu Sound, let us each try to remember:

We don't want to learn anything new. We only want to discover, to hear, that which is always here.

*

*From the unreal lead me to the real,*
*From darkness lead me to light,*
*From death lead me to immortality.*

*(Brihadaranyaka-Upanishad)*

26

*That is perfect. This is perfect. Perfect comes from perfect.*
*Take perfect from perfect, the remainder is perfect.*
*May peace and peace and peace be everywhere.*

As we start our enquiry into any religion—and in this case into the Hindu religion—we must ask ourselves:

What am I hoping to find out?

What do I hope that an understanding of this religion will contribute to me?

What do I want?

What am I looking for?

Am I looking for something to "believe in"?; for a "faith"?; for a "way of life"?

Do I feel myself to be incomplete; lacking in understanding; not fulfilled?

And who is this "I" who is doing this wanting and looking and feeling?

Who am I?

What can the reading of mysterious and ancient scriptures, full of strange and unfamiliar words, have to do with me, now, here—whoever and wherever that may be?

*

Again let us consider the act of listening—and, in particular, listening to *sound* as opposed to *words*.

Mind would make *meaning* out of words; but mind can become *quiescent* through sound.

Now, this is important; mind requires a focus.

If we were to shut ourselves in a soundproof cell would the mind become silent? It would have nothing to listen to—but would it be silent?

Or would it be filled with thoughts, with "thinking"?

And how do thoughts manifest themselves in the mind?

Do we not *hear* them? Do we not *listen* to them?

28

Are we ever free from the sounds, the busy sounds, of our thinking? Ideas and opinions and beliefs, forming as "thoughts" in the mind, chasing each other round and round in a continuous, noisy dance.

When are they not there?

When we are asleep? Is this the only relief that we ever have from them?

Where do thoughts "go to" when we are asleep? Why are they not there? We can sleep in a room full of sounds; we can fall asleep while listening to music, or to somebody speaking, and, when asleep, we cease to hear the sounds any more.

But is this not also true when we are awake?

Then also we can be listening to something, a thought can occur to us, and we can "wander off" in pursuit of that thought in our mind . . . and later, we can start listening again and discover that we have not heard what was being said, or the music being played . . . and so on.

If someone says to me "Now this is important; concentrate" . . . what do I do?

Do I not attempt to focus attention upon that which is said to be important, to the exclusion of all other external sounds or internal thoughts? And do I not very often find that I am so busy listening to the thought "this is important, I must concentrate" that I do not hear the very thing that I am supposed to be concentrating upon?

At such a time the mind is far from quiescent—for it is actively trying to listen.

"There is meaning here," it thinks. "I must make meaning out of these sounds." And it is so busy trying to do just that—that it scarcely hears anything at all!

But how can the mind *try* to listen, when its passive function is that of a "receiver"—a "listener"?

Does mind create ideas—or do ideas "come into mind"?

Mind, we say, "interprets ideas". (*Interpret*: to explain the meaning of, to elucidate, unfold, show the purpose of: to translate into intelligible or familiar terms . . .) But where does it get its ideas

29

from? They "come into it", it "hears them". And to "hear them", it has to be focused, to be listening. That is what it is always doing—listening. But to hear clearly or precisely we need to *attend*, and you cannot give complete attention to two or more different sounds at the same time—unless those sounds "blend" as in a musical chord, in which case the union of the sounds becomes *one sound* for the listener.

Thus, mind, which is always listening, requires *focus*.

How similar this seems to a radio. You switch the radio on—and then you "tune it" to the wavelength or station of your choice. As you approach that station you may get interference from other neighbouring stations—i.e., from stations on or near the wavelength that you are seeking—but you continue to tune the radio until the only sound that it is receiving is that transmitted upon the precise wavelength of your choice.

A radio, being switched on and in good working order—being, as it were "alive"—may be tuned to any station on its waveband, and once it is finely tuned, it will receive whatever is being transmitted on that wavelength.

This analogy may be directly applied to the mind.

If I am "alive" then mind is "switched on".

To "tune" mind you must simply "attend" to a particular subject or sound.

"*To attend*: to wait on: to accompany: to be present at: to wait for . . ."

Perhaps when we are asleep it is not, as we usually think, that "mind is switched off" so much as that there is *no thing* being transmitted that is essential. (Let us leave dreams to one side, for the moment.)

Before we leave the mind radio analogy, let us consider one more aspect of its relevance to *The Question of Religion*.

There are radios—invented, don't let us forget, by the ingenuity of man—of varying strengths. Some can only pick up messages or sounds within a very limited area; others are capable of "hearing" sounds from the other side of the world; there are radio telescopes receiving impulses from across vast distances of what we call "the outer regions of space": it all depends upon the power of the instrument.

What is the ultimate power or strength of *mind* as a receiver?

By posing the question we may see that we do not know the answer.

Is there a limit to *mind* as a receiver or to the impulses which it will interpret as ideas?

Surely the limit must be where the receiver of the impulses and the generator of the impulses *meet*?

Beyond that point lies the unknown.

\*

It is said that the age that we are all living in now is "The Age of Science" or "The Scientific Age".

"*Science*: knowledge ascertained by observation and experiment, critically tested, systematized and brought under general principles . . ."

It is an age in which we—mankind—are seeking for the answers to vast and intangible questions. Yes, it may always have been so; and certainly it is presumptuous to suppose that generations yet unborn will not continue to search, but we are here now, and can only speak for ourselves.

As the scientist, the physicist, the bio-chemist, pit their wits against the outer reaches of cognizable data—each locked onto the precise wavelength of their own particular station, or subject— where does mankind, each and every one of us, stand? For the specialist is a product of his environment, of the climate and corporate being of his age, conditioned by his learning, as each of us is, similarly, a product of this age.

But "cognizable data" is a continuous experience—each answer leads, inevitably, to another question.

The "unknown" has been the carrot that has drawn generation upon generation since the mind began to function.

Before scientific *exposition* became the criteria by which we lived, religious or philosophical *belief* served the same purpose.

Mind has continually been tuned to its apparent limit and then has acknowledged that "there must be something beyond".

During the great "Religious Age" that "something" became a *deity*; the "unknown" was worshipped.

How can *mind* tune in to the "unknown", to the "unmanifest"? Is the radio receiving when it is switched on and yet silent?

This *silence* became the centre of religious life—for, what was there *before* sound?

But mind cannot function without something to listen to. The "silence", the "unknown" was interpreted as GOD—and mind was active again, making from no thing, some thing.

But what was mind originally *hearing*? What was mind originally *listening to*?

What *sound* is there in *silence*?

Meanwhile, mankind was accumulating a vast store of learning from its corporate experience of life.

Gradually *science* was superseding the earlier concept of the unknown as contained in *religion*.

Whereas innumerable generations had trusted in the "unknown" as *God*, now Man was emerging as a being who claimed God-like comprehension.

"I think—therefore, I am."

But—

Who *thinks*?

*Who am I*?

The Scientific Age will continue to probe the mysteries of creation in all its manifestations, and it is as well to remember that no age ends and another begins in a neat, cut-and-dried moment . . . rather, they merge.

For a while religion and philosophy have apparently been abandoned in favour of a new "God"—provable, scientific *fact*.

But facts always point the way to other facts—will there be no end to the chain of discoveries?

Once the *atom* was finite. Then the atom was "split"; the nucleus of protons and neutrons, with electrons buzzing round the nucleus, became the new finite: now we are told, or it is suggested, that the proton contains three quarks . . .

Will there be no end?

32

And, to the lay-person, what *on earth* does it all mean!

Sometimes it seems like a game that the scientists dreamed up to confuse we lesser mortals.

But is it?

Why should intelligent, hard-working, sometimes brilliant members of the human race be playing games with intelligence? That doesn't seem reasonable, does it?

Surely their discoveries *are* valid—even if they only lead, constantly, to yet another enigma, to yet another question?

\*

The scientist, belonging to the Age of Science, working in an area of hypothesis, seeks for provable *fact*.

But what is he looking *for*?

What answers does he seek?

Does he not seek to know:

Who am I?

Where did I come from?

Why am I here?

\*

And the man of religion (would we call him a "religionist"?) living in the great Age of Religion (and we will find that that age had an apparent duration in historic time), what was he looking *for*?

What answers did he seek?

Did he not wish to know:

Who am I?

Where did I come from?

Why am I here?

\*

Then why should not the present draw upon the wisdom of the ages, in the same way that the past may be enhanced by the knowledge of today?

If the Age of Science and the Age of Religion were to marry— what a remarkable Age their offspring could be.

And that Age could be our "today"—The Age of Wisdom.

So, living as we do in the Scientific Age, let us seek for the *sound* of the Age of Religion.

More precisely, let us listen to the ancient, most ancient, wisdom of the *Vedas*.

＊

*Speech, eyes, ears, limbs, life, energy, come to my help. These books have Spirit for theme. I shall never deny Spirit, nor Spirit deny me. Let me be in union, communion with Spirit. When I am one with Spirit, may the laws of these books proclaim live in me, may the laws live.*

*(Kena-Upanishad)*

＊

Any religion is but a mockery unless, given my desire to know, it helps me to understand who I am, to understand the universe, and to understand how the two are related.

How can the Vedic tradition enable me to do this?

Where do I start?

Where?

With I myself, here and now.

＊

What do I want?

The Vedic tradition says that I want three things—happiness, knowledge and immortality. (And it is suggested that these are not really three separate things, but that they are inextricably inter-dependent; it is just that our thinking tends to divide experience.)

A fair statement?

Consider it.

When I look into what I want, and therefore what motivates my actions, I find that, directly or indirectly, all my desire is related to one of these three principles (given that "immortality" can also be read as "wanting never to die").

And can these three "wants" or "desires" be attained—in fulness?

34

Yes, the Vedas tells me—for he or she who is prepared to make certain effort.

What effort?

To explore, understand and abide by "self-knowledge".

He or she who willingly and honestly undertakes this "exploration" is said to have taken the first step on the "Way" or the "Path".

*

In Vedic terms, the Way or the Path implies that a developing (self-developing) understanding informs an evolving self-controlled mode of behaviour.

Evolving towards what?

Towards one purpose—fulfilment, salvation, liberation, realization (and, again, these four may at first seem to have different connotations for each of us but, ultimately, they are only words that describe the same experience).

These words imply knowledge of the full stature and worth of the human being and his or her potential, and are not just worldly terms.

*

It would be highly presumptuous to suggest that we can indicate in a short book the understanding that a man acquires through years and years of observation, study and practice. If it were simply a case of being able to "tell the truth", here, now, in some book—and by that we mean the truth, the whole truth and nothing but the truth— then, presumably, we would all have been "liberated" long ago and all our problems would not even exist, or could be dispelled overnight! But that is not so. The emphasis is always on the individual having to search for the truth for himself or herself—*to realize it (make it real) in his or her own mind*.

This is one of the reasons why Hinduism seems so diffuse, undefinable, flexible, non-exclusive and tolerant; and why it has no laid-down doctrine or common pattern of belief and practice. The emphasis has always been on the individual "choosing and finding his own god", according to his or her own nature, and, although there are temples for communal worship, traditional gods, and public ceremonies for the masses, worship for the Hindu is very much a private concern and his religious life revolves around worship in his own home, in a place set aside for the purpose, without a mediating priest.

This is a fundamentally different approach to the orthodox practice in faith-religions—where obedience to, and worship of, the one god and his law, supervised by an official representative of that god, is sufficient to ensure eternal life, after death.

Although we may not be able to penetrate this Hindu approach very deeply in a single book, some of the ideas expressed in the following chapters may serve as an introduction and will perhaps convey that this ancient "philosophy of life" has something extremely important to contribute to the present human situation . . . to *us*, *now*.

And, it must be added, the Vedic tradition speaks to each one of us in its own way according to our individual nature and therefore this essay must carry the particular preferences and interpretations of the authors. You may hear a different sound, or the sound may be interpreted differently by you. But does that really matter? It is the hearing that is important—and we can only each hear for ourselves.

Furthermore, it ought to be borne in mind that the texts quoted are translations. We have to allow that the English language may not be rich or flexible enough to cope with the nuances of meaning inherent in the sound and structure of Sanskrit.

(It is interesting to note that the translators have used a *poetic* style—and does not poetry, more than any other language form as we know it, depend upon sound, meter and imagery to convey content or meaning?)

We must trust that the translations will be able to convey enough to be worth our "listening to".

Their value must lie in the degree to which they can illuminate our own experience. Only in this way may they lead the individual to realization of Truth (as opposed to becoming just another of the ever-changing and relative truths or valuations by which men commonly live).

*

36

So . . . my search is through "self-knowledge" and it leads to "self-realization" or "liberation". It could be said that the former label would appeal to one who responds and works predominantly with his "head" and the latter to one who responds and works predominantly with his "heart".

But, always, the central focus, the attention or tuning of the question of religion—the heart of "knowing thy self"—must be:

"Who am I?"

\*

*The enquirer asked: "What has called my mind to the hunt? What has made my life begin? What wags in my tongue? What God has opened eye and ear?"*

*The teacher answered: "It lives in all that lives, hearing through the ear, thinking through the mind, speaking through the tongue, seeing through the eye. The wise man clings neither to this nor that, rises out of sense, attains immortal life.*

*"Eye, tongue, cannot approach it nor mind know; not knowing, we cannot satisfy enquiry. It lies beyond the known, beyond the unknown. We know through those who have preached it, have learnt it from tradition.*

*"That which makes the tongue speak, but needs no tongue to explain, that alone is Spirit; not what sets the world by the ears.*

*"That which makes the mind think, but needs no mind to think, that alone is Spirit; not what sets the world by the ears.*

*"That which makes the eye see, but needs no eye to see, that alone is Spirit; not what sets the world by the ears.*

*"That which makes the ear hear, but needs no ear to hear, that alone is Spirit; not what sets the world by the ears.*

*"That which makes life live, but needs no life to live, that alone is Spirit; not what sets the world by the ears."*

\*

*"If you think that you know much, you know little. If you think that you know It from study of your own mind or of nature, study again."*

*The enquirer said: "I do not think that I know much, I neither say that I know, nor say that I do not."*

*The teacher answered: "The man who claims that he knows, knows nothing; but he who claims nothing, knows.*

*"Who says that Spirit is not known, knows; who claims that he knows, knows nothing. The ignorant think that Spirit lies within "knowledge, the wise man knows It beyond knowledge.*

*"Spirit is known through revelation. It leads to freedom. It leads to power. Revelation is the conquest of death.*

*"The living man who finds Spirit, finds Truth. But if he fail, he sinks among fouler shapes. The man who can see the same Spirit in every creature, clings neither to this nor that, attains immortal life."*

*(Kena-Upanishad)*

\*

## THE HINDU SOUND

When was it first recorded?
Who listened to it?
What are its origins?
The "ageless wisdom" which gave rise to the written Vedas was known as *Sanatana Dharma* ("Eternal Law"). It was also known as *Arya Dharma* because, mistakenly, it was thought that the "law" originated at the time of the Aryan arrival in north-west India between 2000 BC and 1500 BC. (It is now suggested that the Aryan nomads came as peaceful immigrants rather than hostile invaders.) In fact, what appears to have happened is that the Vedic knowledge was first written down as scripture in Sanskrit during the period of absorption of the Aryan influence into the already-existing culture of the Indus Valley.

\*

As a result of archaeological investigation, it seems that the Indus Valley civilization was highly developed over four thousand years ago. Artefacts found in excavations indicate that these pre-Aryans principally worshipped the "female" power, associating it particularly with "Mother Earth". This is not surprising as agrarian communities tend to place emphasis on fertility of the earth, a fertility which is crucial to their survival through the cycles of succeeding years. They also, apparently, recognized the importance of the "male" power and that seems to have been represented, in association with fire, by the giver of fertility, a god who seems to be the precursor of the later Shiva (in whom we see the twofold aspect of "fire", both life-giver and destroyer). They also, in this context, acknowledged the role played by the sun, a principal which they represented by the symbol of the *swastika* ("well-being").

This "earth-mother" and "fire" worship, and the emphasis on fertility, played an important part in later developments and they are evident in the ethos of modern India.

On the other hand, the Aryan immigrants evidently placed emphasis on the "gods of the sky" (Varuna, god of the sky; Ushas, goddess of the dawn . . .). This suggests that they preferred to acknowledge the powers to which they were subject as being "unseen"—perhaps we could say more ethereal, or celestial, or beyond the immediate, tangible world.

It is difficult to disentangle at this distance in time which gods and symbols belonged to which culture and what the particular concepts and beliefs actually were; but there seems enough evidence to suggest that in the meeting of the Aryan and the Indus cultures there was, as it were, "a marriage of heaven and earth".

Whatever the nature of their meeting, it undoubtedly represented an exceptional "fertilization", for out of it arose the development of an extraordinarily rich language, Sanskrit, (which means, approximately, "a making together") through which they were able to formulate and write down the Vedic scriptures.

The "core" of the Vedas is what we call "hymns" addressed to gods and goddesses. But we must be careful to note two things:

Firstly, as we have already suggested, these "hymns" were not originally written down, but were only sung, and thus passed from generation to generation verbally—that is to say, they were *listened to* and *learned by heart* by each aspirant. The hymns contained knowledge and, as chanted, were called *Sruti* which means "that which is heard or revealed". Now this, we may surmise, was extremely important because it was not so much the meaning of the words that mattered but the *spoken sound* (and, of course, in translation, we have no idea of the original Sanskrit "sound"). This has to be emphasized because today so much importance is attached to intellectual meanings that we tend not to realize or hear the quality, rhythm and effect of the human *sound*. And we should also not ignore the possibility that the "changeless" *Sruti* is not some primitive system of chanting but that it represents the fact that revelation through sound is an eternal and ever-present possibility for anyone who is minded to *listen*. It is recognition of this that persists today in the use by Indian traditions (and others) of much chanting and of rhythmic sounds (called *mantras*).

Secondly; we should not lightly assume that originally what we now think of as "gods and goddesses" were then conceived of as anthropomorphic deities and were worshipped as "supermen and superwomen". We ought to allow that the images were symbolic and were really understood as simply representations of "powers" and manifest forms of those "powers". This is suggested, for example, in the fact that the gods and goddesses tended to be images of non-human forms and abstract concepts—earth, fire, dawn, light, sky, sun, actual and mythical creatures, and the powers of creativity, fertility, continuity or preservation, destruction or dissolution . . . This is very important because we must allow (as many archaeologists, historians or anthropologists would not) that the essence of this acknowledgement would be to understand and accept divine laws, and was not necessarily worship *of* or *to* some thing.

For example, you may carry about or have framed the photograph of someone dear to you who is absent; if you take the photograph and look at it, it does not mean that you are worshipping that image; you are using it to recollect every possible nuance of the experience of the actual presence of that person. It would be mistaken presumption if some anthropologist of the future were to say, "In the twentieth century, the people often worshipped paper images"!

It is not easy for us to enter into this "state of mind". We might well label such worship "primitive" or "superstitious", and think that our forms of object-worship are far more sophisticated and advanced! A modern theologian might well disapprove of this "idol" worship and call it "impersonal" in contrast to his "personal god". Certainly they were "impersonal" in the sense that they were non-human—but, we might consider, they may well have been highly "personal" in the root sense of that word, "through sound". Perhaps they understood sound in a way that is commonly quite lost to us. Their understanding may have been intensely personal in the sense that they realized that the Ultimate—"God" perhaps—was (and always will be) an inner, formless, individual realization.

\*

The "hymns" of the Vedas, then, were sung or chanted, especially by the holy men or priests, and they were related to specific times of the day, the month and the year. And they were sounded in association with specific rituals, especially "sacrifice" (not necessarily in the common connotation of "blood-letting", but in the real meaning of the word—"making holy"). Hence, the Vedas are divided into four parts—the hymns of praise, the rituals, the explanations of the rituals, and philosophical discourses.

It is these discourses—known as the *Vedanta* (*anta* meaning "end") and called the *Upanishads*—which have attracted much attention in the West, with its predilection for "philosophy".

\*

So, during this period in the Indian continent, say from about 2000 BC to 500 BC, we do not have something that we would readily call a "religion" in the sense that we would associate it with "worship of God". Certainly there was the element of worship (in the sense described above, one of "making oneself worthy") but very much integrated with "love of knowledge" (philosophy) and "knowledge of the mind" (psychology).

Nowadays we tend to separate religion, philosophy and psychology into three "disciplines", but, if we look into them deeply, *in relationship with experience*, we may well discover that they are mutually dependent and inseparable. Indeed, they almost become synonymous.

In Vedic terms, the three aspects are inextricably woven together in the human search for, and realization of, the Ultimate Reality or Truth.

*

It is not easy to speculate and summarize what then happened in the Vedic development but we can imagine that the search for Ultimate Reality would have become an inspiration for only a minority of the population (just as an increasing majority of the world today is not vitally interested in orthodox religion). As the population grew, we may assume that the mass of people would have become increasingly unaware of, or not interested in, the essence of the Vedic teaching.

And so, gradually, there would have developed a "personalization" of the gods and goddesses, worship *of* them as "super-persons", habitual performance of superstitious ritual and sacrifice as oblation *to* the deities, and hence the growth of dogma. According to personal preference and particular influences of family and community, different people began to worship and champion different deities, and the integrated body of knowledge dispersed into a multitude of separated creeds, doctrines and beliefs.

*

In parallel with this (presumed) process of "personalization", there arose a second category of scripture, called *Smriti* (as distinct from *Sruti*), which means "re-interpretation" or "recollection", and it is said that it arose through the necessity to "adapt to changing conditions". Thus, over a period of about fifteen hundred years beginning two and a half thousand years ago, there appeared the "popularization" of the Vedic tradition in the form of tales, stories and myths. The two great epic poems of this period were the *Ramayana* and the *Mahabharata*, and it is in the latter that is found the *Bhagavad-Gita* ("The Lord's Song" or "The Song of God") which contains the essence of the Upanishadic "philosophy" in the form of a discourse between Krishna, an incarnation of the god Vishnu, and Arjuna, a mortal prince.

\*

Inevitably, at the same time as the development of this personalization and popularization of the Vedic tradition, there arose those who considered that the essence of the teaching was being misinterpreted and lost, and who attempted to "purify", redefine and retrieve. This gave rise to many sects and movements, including Buddhism and Jainism.

\*

Perhaps we should pause here for a moment and look at a wider perspective. During this period, the "personalization" of religion was a widespread phenomenon in the world—as if mankind as a whole was psychologically entering a new era.

Within a period of one millennium (say 600 BC to AD 600—what we have termed "The Religious Age"), there appeared the great "personalities" who "founded" the religions and schools of thought which have so strongly influenced the course of human history to this day—most notably Gautama Buddha, Lao Tze, Confucius, Socrates, Plato, Zarathustra, Jesus of Nazareth and the Prophet, Mohammed.

Is it not extraordinary that all these outstanding men of influence should have appeared in such a relatively short time—and that no one of such stature in the realms of religion and philosophy has appeared since? (True, there have been many notable "thinkers" and "theologians"—but they have been reformers, adapters, developers, modifiers, and not "originators".)

And to put our present subject into perspective, we must appreciate that the Vedic scriptures were as remote in the past to, say, Jesus, as Jesus, the historical figure, is remote to us now.

\*

Whatever the significance in the overall, final "destiny of man" of the appearance of this wealth of inspiration at that time, we can

43

see there the "seeds" of what have become the world's great faith-religions. The implication of the word "faith" is that a vast proportion of civilized humanity entered an era of believing in, and worshipping, a "personal god".

In the areas influenced at that time by the Vedic tradition, there developed a period called "the age of *bhakti*", which means a period of devotion and worship (of all manner of "god-images"). And when the Muslim emperors invaded the north-west of the Indian continent (from about AD 1000) they called this multitude of forms of creed and worship, after their first contacts in the region of the Indus river, *Hindu*. (Later, due to the West's penchant for categorizing any form of thought an "ism", we arrived at the word "Hinduism").

So . . . it can be appreciated that "Hinduism" is a complex and probably indefinable term and that it is impossible to say that, as a religion, it stands specifically for "this" or "that" ideology or belief.

Statistically we may know that there are over four hundred million Hindus today, mostly in the Far East. But "Hindu" is a term with little integrity and cohesion, for it embraces all manner of apparent contradictions and irreconcilables—polytheism and monotheism, personal gods and impersonal principles, simplicity and complexity, contrasts of austerity and indulgence, advocacy of sexuality and celibacy, and so on. As opposed to say Christianity or Buddhism, Hinduism has no founder, no "personality" or teacher whose words and deeds form a central focus or reference point.

Today, the image often presented to the world by Hinduism is alien to the science and technology of "developed", industrial societies. The idols, the multi-armed and multi-faced gods, the stylized demons and spirits, the river ablutions and riverside cremations in public, the chanting and racket of *puja* (religious ceremonies) can seem, at best, quaint and colourful, at worst, primitive, superstitious and far removed from the respect and reverence one would perhaps expect of man in communion with the divine.

Thus, in view of our proposition that the key for us lies in the original Vedic scriptures (despite their distance from us in time and the fact that we have to make do with translations) and, in particular, what they "say" to the individual who "silently listens", we have preferred to avoid the word "Hinduism" and have chosen for this book the title *The Hindu Sound*.

The writings may be strange to us, we may at times find them baffling and obscure—but, if we do, it is pretty certain that we are trying too hard to understand their *meaning* and striving to make *sense* of the *words*. Behind the words, containing the words, is the *sound*, and the *sound*, while telling a story or revealing Truth, requires only that the mind should *attend* and *rest*.

*

*Once upon a time, Spirit planned that the gods might win a great victory. The gods grew boastful; though Spirit had planned their victory, they thought they had done it all.*

*Spirit saw their vanity and appeared. They could not understand; they said: "Who is that mysterious Person?"*

*They said to Fire: "Fire! Find out who is that mysterious Person."*

*Fire ran to Spirit. Spirit asked what it was. Fire said: "I am Fire; known to all."*

*Spirit asked: "What can you do?" Fire said: "I can burn anything and everything in this world."*

*"Burn it," said Spirit, putting a straw on the ground. Fire threw itself upon the straw, but could not burn it. Then Fire ran to the gods in a hurry and confessed it could not find out who was that mysterious Person.*

*Then the gods asked Wind to find out who was that mysterious Person.*

*Wind ran to Spirit and Spirit asked what it was. Wind said: "I am Wind; I am King of the Air."*

*Spirit asked: "What can you do?" and Wind said: "I can blow away anything and everything in this world."*

*"Blow it away," said Spirit, putting a straw on the ground. Wind threw itself upon the straw but could not move it. Then Wind ran to the gods in a hurry and confessed it could not find out who was that mysterious Person.*

45

*Then the gods went to Light and asked it to find out who was that mysterious Person. Light ran towards Spirit, but Spirit disappeared upon the instant.*

*There appeared in the sky that pretty girl, the Goddess of Wisdom, snowy Himalaya's daughter. Light went to her and asked who was that mysterious Person.*

*The Goddess said: "Spirit, through Spirit you attained your greatness. Praise the greatness of Spirit." Then Light knew that the mysterious Person was none but Spirit.*

*That is how these gods—Fire, Wind and Light—attained supremacy; they came nearest to Spirit and were the first to call that Person Spirit.*

*Light stands above Fire and Wind; because closer than they, it was the first to call that Person Spirit.*

*This is the moral of the tale. In the lightning, in the light of the eye, the light belongs to Spirit.*

*The power of the mind when it remembers and desires, when it thinks again and again, belongs to Spirit. Therefore let Mind meditate on Spirit.*

*(Kena-Upanishad)*

\*

The word "meditate" is often misused in the West. We liken it to "think".

"Thinking" and "meditation" are as different as "dark" is to "light".

We think *about*, but we meditate *on*.

Mind, in meditation, *rests on* the object—or, more specifically, the *sound*.

We must consider *meditation* in more detail later—for as the Vedas carry the "message", so the mind, resting, quiescent in meditation, is tuned to hear.

If the Vedas are the structure, meditation is the foundation.

\*

To speculate as to the meaning of the many forms of the Hindu religion—and the performance of it—may be interesting as a study;

46

but if I am wanting to understand the meaning of "religion" itself, then such study will be idle and useless and will only be another collection of learning. If I am a "practising" Hindu, then of course I need to consider what it is that I am performing; if I am not, then it is for me to judge how valid or invalid such performance may be. What I need to know—whatever the system of thought or religion I have been introduced to in my society—is whether *any* teaching, whatever its orgin, can help me to understand what it means *to be religious*.

Religion—any religion—must be a means; never an end. We do not know the "end". We can only be here now.

Through the wisdom of the Vedas we may hear the whisper of that sound that first prompted our deepest questions. For wisdom is not exclusive; it is every man's birthright. It does not depend upon education, nor luck; it depends only upon discrimination, the fine tuning of attention, and the magnitude of the desire in the individual to discover his or her *Self*.

*

*Spirit is the Good in all. It should be worshipped as the Good. He that knows it as the Good is esteemed by all.*

*You asked me about spiritual knowledge, I have explained it.*

*Austerity, self-control, meditation are the foundations of this knowledge; the Vedas are its house, truth its shrine.*

*He who knows this shall prevail against all evil, enjoy the Kingdom of Heaven, yes, for ever enjoy the blessed Kingdom of Heaven.*

(*Kena-Upanishad*)

*Therefore let Mind meditate on Spirit*

How far, I wonder, can we take the mind/radio analogy?

Just consider the words in the above sentence!

What is this capacity—peculiar to mind—"to wonder"?

The word "wonder" in the English language is used for a number of widely differing "meanings".

*Wonder*: a miracle; a strange and remarkable thing . . . wonderful . . . what a wonder . . . no wonder . . . a wonder of creation . . .

*Wonder*: Emotion excited by what surpasses expectation or experience or seems inexplicable; surprise mingled with admiration or curiosity or bewilderment . . . filled with wonder . . . looked at (it) with silent wonder . . . open-mouthed wonder . . . struck dumb with wonder . . .

*Wonder*: wonderland; fairyland . . .

*Wonder*: be filled with wonder . . . feel surprise . . .

*Wonder*: curiosity, leading to a desire to know . . . wonder why pain exists . . . wonder what time it is . . .

How far, I wonder, can we take the mind/radio analogy? . . .

I wonder what "wonder" means?

*

Hopefully, you know what I am trying to express, but, nevertheless, it does seem a rather hit-or-miss situation when one word can be interpreted in innumerable different ways!

It could be argued that the word—any word—depends upon the words it is related to . . .

But:

How far, I wonder, can we take the mind/radio analogy?

Am I—the speaker/writer—*curious* when I ask the question and therefore anxious to continue the discussion? Or am I *bewildered*, and hinting that it is about time to call a halt to this line of enquiry? Am I *amazed*, *excited*, *admiring*, or even, possibly *shocked* at the question? "I wonder at it, I really do!"

*

For you to be sure, really *sure*, of what I am endeavouring to say in this situation, you would have to *hear* me *say* it; and, in *hearing*

49

me, you would have to be "tuned" to pick-up the subtle implications of *emotion* contained in the tone, meter, pitch . . . the *sound* of my voice.

Clearly this is not possible, for you are *reading* these words and there is no *sound* reaching you from the originator of them—i.e., the writer.

There is no sound except, possibly, the sound of the read words in your head?

*

(Here is an interesting game-exercise:

*Now*, as you are silently reading these words on this page . . . how are the words "entering your mind"? Do they manifest as spoken, albeit silent, sounds? "In other words", are you "hearing" the words that you're "seeing"? How is the "seeing" being translated into "meaning", into "form" . . . and, eventually, into an "understanding"?

It's a game worth playing.

Look up, now, from the page.

What did you see? How was the "seeing" seen? . . .)

*

For you to be sure, really *sure*, of what I am endeavouring to *say*, the language that I use should be absolutely precise (precise: precut) so that each word can only mean what *I* intend it to mean.

*

In the Vedic tradition it is said that:

"Words mean what they do . . ."

And the "words", before they were ever written down in the precisely evolved Sanskrit language (Sanskrit: a word itself, formed from *sam*, "together" and *kr*, "make": "together-make") were *sounds*.

This concept: of a *sound* meaning what it *does*, is very far reaching.

(For example: in the Christian tradition, it can shed light on the opening of St. John's Gospel:

"In the beginning was the *Word* . . ."

It seems to suggest that the first impulse in all creation . . . was *sound* . . .)

*

Language as we know it today, particularly in the more techno-cratic societies, is becoming increasingly complex. New words are continually coming into the vernacular to describe new experiences, new discoveries; the jargon of the scientist, the astro-physicist, the psychiatrist, the economist, the politician . . . an ever-increasing morass of gobbledegook . . . unless you happen to think you already know the meaning of the particular words! Meanwhile our everyday language becomes increasingly vague and imprecise. "I wonder what 'wonder' means?" . . . The word "nice" in the English language can mean "pleasant" and it can mean "scrupulous".

"He's a nice person." What do you mean by that?

How often have we picked up a book, or listened to someone speak, on a subject that we are anxious to understand—simply to abandon the endeavour moments later simply because "we do not know what the person is talking about"? We *want* to understand—they want to be understood . . . but we cannot get past the barrier of unfamiliar language.

Words, at such times, cease to *do* what is required of them (to inform) because all the emphasis has been concentrated upon the analysis of their *meaning*.

But a word is only a series of *sounds* . . . those sounds do not *mean* anything: their meaning has been given to them.

This isn't so complex as it sounds!

Listen now to a favourite piece of music—or, if that is not possible at the moment, listen to a bird singing. No bird? Turn on the tap—and listen to the water flowing. Listen to the breeze. Listen to your breathing.

Or, just clap your hands together.

Now—*clap your hands*.

*

Did that sound have, of itself, any meaning?

51

Mind may say: "Yes, it meant my hands were being clapped together."

But—did it? Or did you not *give it* that meaning?

*Clap your hands together.*

There was a sound—and it did something.

It didn't *mean* anything other than what it *did*.

*

This is not just a form of "mental gymnastics"; it is the beginning of a journey into the complex nature of mind. Your mind—or, your concept of your mind? We shall see.

It is the first step on a journey *through* mind.

It is the beginning of self-knowledge.

*

MIND

"I mind . . ."

"I don't mind . . ."

"I re-mind you . . ."; "You re-mind me . . ."

"In mind . . . 'absent-minded . . .' 'out of my mind . . .' 'never mind'!"

Mind: a word I use a great deal—and yet, do I have any comprehension as to what I mean when I use it?

"Mind" as distinct from "body"?

"Mind"—where my thinking goes on?

"Mind"—something to do with my brain?

*

The nature of what we mean by this word, when we use it, is something that we must explore if we are to have any idea about ourselves.

For, "As I think, so I am".

*

Where is "mind"?

How "big" is it?

If I have one, where did it come from and where did I obtain it? What is it made of?

I speak about "my mind" but, in what respect do I have it or possess it?

AND, here is a problem . . . whatever I think or decide about mind, it will be mind thinking and deciding it!

Yet . . . I *know* the mind is thinking it—so, who am *I* who knows what is being thought?

*

Let us try another practical experiment—a game, if you like:
Read through the following sentences:
Sit comfortably and close your eyes.
Listen.
Just that— listen.
There are sounds near to you.
Let the listening "go out" to them.
Just listen to those sounds.
Now—do what the words have suggested you should do.

*

While you were listening to those sounds, did you "contain" them?

Were the sounds "outside" you . . . or did they, somehow, seem to be "inside" you—or rather, "in mind"?

Concentrating on the experience of the sound, is it honestly true to say that "you" were *separate* from the sound?

In this experience of listening, did you not, in a strange way, become the sound . . . or the sound became "a part of you"?

Then there was only the sound.

*

Try it again.
Listen.
Just listen to the near sounds.
Listen.

*

In the moment of listening, the listener and the sound are joined as one.

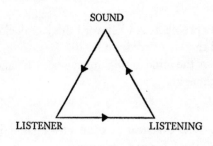

*

Let us take the experiment a stage further.
Listen again.
This time beyond the near sounds.
Listen to the distant sounds.
Are there more distant sounds still?
Let the listening go out to them and "contain" them . . .

*

In a fraction of a moment, were "you" not then at the farthest sound?
Does it matter that the intellect tells you that the sound is feet away or miles away?
In willing the listening to "go out" to the sound, the mind, as it were, "expanded in space" and contained that sound. In the experience of *listening* to that sound, the matter of its so-called "distance away" from "you" was meaningless.
Was it like that?
We can only be sure if we each try the experiment.
It is not enough to read such a statement here on the page—we must try it each for ourselves—for the *meaning* can only be in the *experiencing*.
The *meaning* is what it *does*—to you, to me.

54

We have been saying that the listening "goes out" to the sound; that is what it "feels" like, even although the action is almost instantaneous.

The scientific "model" of the mechanics of sound and hearing would tell us that something is vibrating and "making a sound"; the sound vibrations are forming pressure waves in the air which in turn vibrate the ear drum and then "somehow" the auditory nerves transmit the form and quality of the sound to the brain where the sound is "experienced" and analysed.

*

But if any of this is correct—then where *is* the sound?
"Out there" or "in the brain"?
Is it "here" or "there"? Or both? Is it "everywhere"?

*

Close your eyes and listen, really listen to any sound.
Enter and rest in that sound.

*

Without prejudice, without *thinking* about "near" or "far away", "here" or "there" . . . did the factor of distance belong to the *experience* at all?

Does it not only come into experience when you *think about* the sound—as though the concept "distance" is superimposed on the experience?

*In* listening, the sound is "everywhere", filling the mind.

It is only afterwards, through the experience and learning of the senses of touch and sight, that the mind constructs or "creates" its "model" of the world and conceives of distance.

(And even now, at this moment, how mind wants to reject such a statement!)

But just consider it!

If a primitive tribe was introduced for the very first time to a radio—where would they say the sound was coming from? What would they say was making the sound?

Ignorant of our concept of radio-waves and transmitters and receivers and so on, would they not believe that the originator of the sound they heard was inside the radio box?

And would they be entirely wrong?

True, they wouldn't find a little person in there, reading the news or whatever! And, yes, of course, they would be bewildered by all the wires and valves, etc. Particularly if, snapping a wire . . . the sound stopped . . .

But—where was the sound?

They were not wrong in believing it came from inside the box—however much an intelligent, learned, person tries to tell them about the *wonders* of radio science!

Were they wrong?

Perhaps they were both right *and* wrong?

Perhaps it all depends upon our model of the world?

\*

In the Vedic tradition, the order of precedence of the "earthly elements" through which mind "creates" its model of the world is:

SPACE, AIR, FIRE, WATER, EARTH . . . in that order.

These five sensible elements are directly linked to the five senses, thus:

| SPACE | — | SOUND |
|-------|---|-------|
| AIR | — | TOUCH |
| FIRE | — | SIGHT |
| WATER | — | TASTE |
| EARTH | — | SMELL |

\*

Why, if I am in a room where there are many sounds, do I not hear all of them at once . . . which presumably I should do if, scientifically speaking, all the sounds are making pressure waves and hence they are all bombarding my eardrums?

Or, again—have you ever experienced sitting in a garden on a warm, summer day? There are birds singing in the trees, but, after a while, engrossed in some conversation or reading or whatever, you cease to hear them. So much so, indeed, that you may well have to make a "conscious effort" to hear them again . . .

Perhaps we could say on such occasions that I am *hearing* all the sounds . . . but I only *listen* to a certain selection of them—or, maybe, only one.

And the distinction between hearing and listening, is that *I choose*, through an act of *will* (though we may not think of it as that at first) to select a particular sound to listen to, and ignore all the others.

*

"*Is there anything above mind?*" *said Narada.*

"*Yes,*" *said Sanatkumar.* "*Will is above mind. When man wills he thinks, calls up speech which breaks into names. Sentences are made out of words, actions are made out of thoughts.*

"*Everything is founded on will; everything forms will; everything lives in will. Heaven and earth will; wind and air will; water and light will; rain wills because water and light will; food wills because rain wills; life wills because food wills; speech wills because life wills; actions will because speech wills; world wills because actions will; everything wills because world wills. Such is will. Worship will.*

"*Who worships will as Spirit, obtains the world he wills, attains the eternal by his will for the eternal, attains honour by his will for honour, attains the sorrowless by his will to go beyond sorrow. Who worships will as Spirit, moves within the limits of what is willed, as it may please him, provided he worships will as nothing but Spirit.*"

"*Is there anything above will?*" *said Narada. . . .*

(*Chhandogya-Upanishad*)

*

Let us try another experiment.

Again, sit comfortably and close the eyes. (Why? So that we are not distracted by another sense—seeing.)

Now

Sense the pressure of your foot on the floor.

57

Now
Sense the tip of the forefinger of your right hand.
Now
Sense the tip of your tongue.
Now
Sense the "area" between your eyes.

*

Try it.
Foot on the ground; tip of the forefinger of the right hand; tip of the tongue; the "area" between your eyes.

*

What moved from one point of the body to another?
What travelled where ("touching by subtle air")?
And—under whose direction or will was it done?

*

You could answer, "The focus of attention was moved" and "I did it".
But—what is "attention" and how is it "moved", how is it "focused on something?
And—where is the "I" who willed it to move from foot to finger to tongue to forehead?

*

These simple exercises can be most revealing.
They may show us how ignorant (in the real sense of "ignoring") we are.
We cannot deny, surely, that we take a great deal for granted.
Why?
For one reason, we are so interested in the mind's interpretation of the world's images and happenings that we rarely, if ever, pause to wonder how mind is doing it. We settle for the scientific explanation of the *result* rather than ponder on *how* the result came to be.

We begin to find that scientific explanations have a definite limitation, because they are only intellect-devised interpretations of experience once it has *taken place*; such interpretations never "explain" *how* the experience *takes* place or *where* the experience originates.

However, for the mind, continually fed with explanations, this approach may seem alien and difficult.

Is it possible, with practice, to "get behind" the façade and *observe* what is actually happening, moment by moment?

Clearly we shall not penetrate the mind deeply without such observation.

And our journey is "through" mind . . .

So, is it possible?

*

In the experimental exercises suggested earlier, what else was observed?

Was the attention "taken" or did I "give" it?

How can I "give" attention to something unless it is already there—and therefore "taking" attention?

If something is not being given, or taking, attention—*is it there*?

In other words, does a thing exist for me, if I do not know that it exists?

*

Let us take another step.

Until I have given something my attention—no matter how little of it—I am not aware of its existence.

As far as my *actual, immediate* experience is concerned, a "thing" cannot, surely, exist for *me*, unless I am aware of it.

Thus, scientific learning will tell me that on a bright summer's afternoon there are stars in the sky . . . but, due to the strength of the sunlight, they cannot be seen.

Which is the truth . . . are the stars there or not?

What is the evidence of my "senses"?

That they are not there.

But my intellect, with its concept of time and sequence and continuity, tells me they *must* be there.

Which is the "reality"?

On a clear night, I see the stars in the sky.

I have been told, and have learned as a "fact", that these stars are "millions of light years" away . . . indeed that many of them may even no longer exist. What I am seeing is light that has been on its way through space for millions of years before striking my eye at this moment, now, and before being named a "star".

But does such explanation make a scrap of difference to my experience?

I look at a star . . . and *immediately* it *is*, "in" my mind-experience . . .

So, how big or how small is my mind?

Where does it "begin" and where does it "end"?

How is it that I can "reach to the stars" if I am so minded?

What *is* going on?

Perhaps we are totally misguided in assuming the mind to be a "thing" at all and perhaps it is utterly irrelevant to speak of it in the terms by which we describe and measure the physical, phenomenal, world?

*

*"Is there anything above will?" said Narada.*

*"Yes," said Sanatkumar. "Mind's mother substance is above will. When that is stirred, man wills; thinks, calls up speech; which breaks forth in words. Sentences are made of names; actions are made of thoughts.*

*"All these are founded on mind's mother substance. They form that substance, they live in substance. Man may be learned in names, but if that substance is absent, he is absent; he is ignored by everybody, the names go for nothing. Everybody listens to a man, no matter how light his learning, if substance be there. Therefore that substance is the abode of all. That substance is Self, is rock. Worship the mind's mother substance.*

*"Who worships that as Spirit, moves within the limits of all that it*

*contains, as it may please him, provided he worships it as nothing but Spirit. He attains the eternal by becoming eternal, he attains the unchanging by becoming unchanging, attains joy, becomes joy."*
*"Is there anything above that substance?" said Narada ...*

*(Chhandogya-Upanishad)*

\*

I shall not penetrate the mind deeply if I happily assume I know what words really mean simply because I have been told their meaning by someone else. I need to experience, for example, what I call "mind", and "will" and "knowledge", not as concepts—but as realities, by me experienced.

\*

The Vedic tradition says the words (as sounds) mean *what they do*.
And now we must consider the precision of the Sanskrit expression of that Vedic tradition.
In Sanskrit there are words for the subtle differences in "meaning".
We need not necessarily *learn* these words—though it will be useful to recognize them so that we may save the time and space of constantly defining their meaning—but it is essential that we should know what they do. In other words, do not worry if you don't remember the word, or name—sense rather what the word does; the meaning that it creates.

\*

Let us now consider one word. The Vedic philosophy calls a belief that something exists in its own right, "outside mind", *maya* or "illusion" (though it must be added, this is only *one* approach or interpretation of the word).
This suggests that in *believing*—or rather, in our coming to believe—the real world to be "out there" (i.e. "outside" the body) the mind has been deceived. (This concept is the equivalent of "the fall" in the Judaic and Christian traditions.)
The delusion takes place because mind "projects" the world as

being "out there" through the ignorance of the intellect in its understanding of the evidence of the senses.

On the other hand, intellect is deluded also in thinking that the world-image is "here" in the brain.

In *reality*, the world *is in mind*:

And mind is dimensionless, mind is timeless.

*

*The Divine Eternal is real, the world is illusion; a complete certainty of this is declared to be Discernment between the Eternal and the non-eternal.*

*(Vivekachudamani—"The Crest Jewel of Wisdom"—attributed to Shankara Acharya)*

*

For, if I think that mind has dimension . . . with what will I measure it?

*

Thus mind wrestles with itself—and a very tiring process it is; as no doubt you, the reader, are discovering!

For now you—and the writers—are encountering difficulty!

Apart from something being proposed which may seem totally alien . . . if not preposterous (given the way in which our minds are conditioned by learning) . . . we, as writers, are once again faced with the limitation of words.

We are challenged with the problem, for example, that we all have assumptions, however vague, about the words we use. Here, now, we assume that we can speak of "mind" and "will" with impunity. "I know my mind." "I know what I want to do." "Of course I have a mind of my own." "Of course I decide what I want to do." And so on . . .

And relatively speaking, we must think like that—otherwise we would be reduced to living as "vegetables"! Of course we have to go about our everyday business, but . . .

In what direction lies the possibility of realizing *what* we are doing, *why* we are doing it? In what direction lies the possibility of penetrating the façade of mind-assumption?

In what direction lies the possibility of becoming *wiser*?

*

"*Is there anything above that substance?*" *said Narada.*

"*Yes,*" *said Sanatkumar.* "*Meditation is above substance. Earth, sky, heaven, water, mountain, men, gods, meditate. The greatness of the great comes from meditation. Small men quarrel, deceive, denounce; great men meditate, enjoy the greatness that it brings. Worship meditation.*

"*Who worships meditation as Spirit, moves within the limits of its subject, as it may please him, provided that he worships meditation as nothing but Spirit.*"

"*Is there anything above meditation?*" *said Narada . . .*

(*Chhandogya-Upanishad*)

Let's have a rest!

Who rests? What rests? How do we rest?

Must we sleep to rest?

What requires to rest—now, at this moment?

Obviously not the body—after all, it has simply been sitting here, reading!

But mind has been active; mind has been working: mind is tired; mind requires a rest.

How do you rest the mind?

Sleeping? Dreaming? Thinking about something else?

## LISTEN TO THE SILENCE

Each time a thought "comes into mind", turn away from it. Let it go. Do not entertain it.

Who "turns away"? Who "lets it go"? Who "does not entertain it"?

Do not, for now, bother about these questions. Do not become involved in them.

## LISTEN TO THE SILENCE

Is there such a "thing"? Is there "silence", ever, "anywhere"?

Just try it—for your own "peace of mind" . . .

## LISTEN TO THE SILENCE

The Vedic knowledge avoids rigid structures, detailed instructions and specific definitions because, we may surmise, the problems and dangers of intellectual misinterpretation were well understood.

It was (and still is) very important in the tradition that there should be a vital teacher-student relationship—between the giver and recipient of the ancient wisdom; a close and dominantly verbal communication because, among many factors, not only could the teacher be certain of the effects of his words and the appropriateness of them in a given circumstance, but he could make sure by continual questioning and discussion that the "disciple" ("one who learns") had not misunderstood the meaning of the words.

It was also acknowledged that there were "levels" of such understanding, which were attained "step by step". It was not simply a case of imparting knowledge or information; the recipient had to be ready to receive it and this would be governed by his "level of being".

It is not easy to describe this concept of "level of being", but it has a lot to do with the degree to which the aspirant (or disciple) sheds erroneous belief and is free from pre-conception and prejudice.

Thus, *understanding* was (and is) related to degree of *knowledge* and degree of *being*.

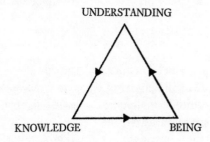

UNDERSTANDING

KNOWLEDGE                    BEING

Translating this into perhaps more familiar terms, we would say that degree of wisdom is not just a matter of greater or lesser learning but the ability of the individual to relate that learning to living—to be able to apply it in practice—to be able to speak and act wisely.

In this sense, we may see the interdependence of psychology, philosophy and religion (in the sense of living a "holier"—"whole" —life).

The Vedic tradition evidently fully recognized and understood this interdependence. The knowledge contained in the scriptures seems total, all-embracing—albeit complex and subtle; yet undeniably profound.

\*

What we would call "ordinary" mind-functioning involves a variety of experience.

It involves, for example, imagining, wandering thoughts, daydreaming, all that activity which suggests idle, uncontrolled, "circling" images and thought-forms.

Then there is what we might call "applied" thought—for example, problem solving, decision making, where some control (or "will") is introduced so that the mind can "work something out" to some purpose . . . with the use of comparison, analysis, logic and so on.

The Vedic tradition would call these, in translation, something like "discursive" mind. This suggests "running off in pursuit of things".

\*

Next, there is that which "conditions" the thinking—the accumulation in "memory" of all manner of stored and maintained concept, belief, prejudice, attitude, opinion . . . based, in turn, upon many different deep desires and fears.

Then there is the immediate information coming through the senses—millions of particular impressions, only a fraction of which attract attention (and some of which a "part" of mind responds to without thought or "me" being aware of them; thus, for example, shifting position of the body to alleviate discomfort, or your eyes, now, scanning across this page).

*

All the above—discursive thinking, memory, sense impressions, etc.—could be called the "contents" of mind.

And a very curious and varied collection it can be!

Undoubtedly, the Vedic sages understood these processes—their nature and constitution, their roles and relative levels of intelligence.

We have only crudely and partially classified them but the point, as far as we are concerned here, is that *all* these mental phenomena were *observed* and objectively understood in relation to one purpose —liberation, salvation, realization, whichever label one cares to choose.

*

Inextricably involved with the mind-forms and their processes, there are what we might call "organs" of mind—the different "parts" of the mind which carry out certain functions.

Again we cannot investigate these in detail but we should mention two which recur in the Vedic scriptures.

The Sanskrit names are:

*Manas* and *Buddhi*.

What do these two words *mean*?

Let us attempt to see what they *do*.

*

*Manas* is essentially to do with the "motion" or "circulation" of the mind. It could be thought of, in one aspect, as being a kind of mediator or "message carrier" (probably commensurate with the Roman "Mercury" or Greek "Hermes", "the messenger of the gods"). However, it would be misleading to try to limit Manas to being a "thing". It is not a substance, a mechanical process—it is not a thing which can be de-graded to physical or mundane terms (any-more than a Hindu, Roman or Greek "god" can with validity be thought of as a "thing").

67

But—we can observe and experience Manas.

We already have in the exercises suggested earlier.

Manas could be observed as that which "carried" the attention—or was itself the attention "travelling"—to the sounds, the foot, the finger . . .

*Buddhi* is often likened to a mirror or reflector—which may be "clean" and "clear" or "dirty" and "confused". Buddhi's power and efficacy is invoked in what we would call "evaluating" or "discriminating". It "holds up for comparison" and plays a crucial role in the clarity or confusion in the act of deciding or choosing. Thus we would "feel" Buddhi failing to operate clearly in those moments of confusion when we are unable to make a choice. Buddhi operates effectively when it *reflects* "certain knowledge" so that we could also consider it as a mediator—transmitting knowledge held in the memory.

*

So, in these two, Manas and Buddhi, we have Manas the presenter or gatherer of information or impression and Buddhi the evaluator of that information or impression—whether it be "messages" coming through the senses or thought-forms or dream-images in the mind—in which process Buddhi reflects the "light" of knowledge, the meaning.

Further, these two—Manas and Buddhi—are the key to "purity" of mind and hence to the aspiring religious life.

But without direction, Manas and Buddhi run riot.

It depends upon what they are serving, and the third crucial factor—whose "will" is served—we must consider very soon.

*

We have suggested that Buddhi evaluates and discriminates clearly with certain knowledge—when it is not confused.

How is Buddhi confused?

Again, this is not easy to penetrate because of the limitation of words, more especially the written word. We tend to use words like "learning", "knowledge" and "wisdom" *indiscriminately* (i.e.

Buddhi is not reflecting clearly the meaning of the words) and inter-change them capriciously . . . say, simply from a point of view of "style", to avoid repetition. But, in Vedic terms, such words are quite distinct in meaning. We have seen, for example, that in the quotation from the *Eesha Upanishad*, at the beginning of this book, the translator has had to use the terms "natural knowledge" and "supernatural knowledge" in an attempt to convey quite different degrees for which our language has no specific words.

How can we establish this point?

Ordinary knowledge is "the learning in, and of, this phenomenal world" and is what we would call "fact". It consists of "explana-tion" of the physical world and is limited by such concepts as chronological time and measurable dimension. It is *finite*.

"Real knowledge" or "supernatural knowledge" is not taught and is not learned; it is innate and transcends scientific fact; it is always immediate and has connotations of eternity and the *infinite*. We would include it in such terms as "instinct" and "intuition" and it is said to be the "heart" of memory. It would range from a plant "knowing" how to grow a flower, a spider "knowing" how to spin a web, a bird "knowing" its song, and so on . . . all the way to the human experience called "conscience" or the undeniable "isness" of "I know that I am". It is a capacity to respond to "the sound of things" ("rea-son") which gives rise to such expressions as "It *sounds* right" (which we especially use when there seems no other criteria available with which to judge something).

This calibre of knowledge—"real knowledge"—is always ex-perienced in the immediate "*now*" (it is not "worked out"). In the moment it is undeniable (though the intellect through its learning may distrust it in "afterthought") and the mind "does not know where it has come from".

Buddhi will reflect clearly in the "light" of this certain knowledge; the sense of confusion arises when there is then a trying to equate that knowledge with incompatible learning—the "dim glow" or "seeing darkly" through conditioning.

Hence, in a simple, mundane example, I might have to choose between a red box and a green box. Due to conditioning I may prefer one colour to the other—and then there is no difficulty in choosing. But suppose I have no preference? Buddhi is confused because the choice has to be made in the absence of conditioned preference and no certain knowledge arises to help in the choice—except that the confusion may be compounded by the certain knowledge that it is utterly immaterial whether I have the red or the green! (As a result, I may try to avoid the issue and say, "I don't *mind* which I have" . . . which is my way of expressing the knowledge that the organ of evaluation has no way of deciding!)

But, of course, it is in far more serious issues that we need to observe this process in action. For example, we may see confusion arise in a situation where "I know what I ought to do" is opposed by "I want to do this instead".

And when we come to appreciate that observation of the activity of Manas and Buddhi is crucial to discrimination between truth and untruth, between the real and illusion—and hence to the growth of wisdom—we will understand the emphasis placed on them by the Vedic tradition.

*

And so, for our exploration in this book, we have introduced Manas and Buddhi as being vital elements in consideration of "mind" and its activity.

Why the emphasis placed on them in the Vedic tradition?

Because, without control and discipline, Manas, the "carrier of attention", is always dashing off all over the place and never rests.

Without control and discipline, Buddhi fails to evaluate and discriminate clearly and is at the mercy of every passing desire and fear.

In this situation, the mind is continually deluded.

*

Under control and direction, attention may be freed by discrimination from involvement in all manner of self-indulgent and useless thinking and behaviour. Attention freed allows the "sphere of consciousness" to expand to the most distant horizon, the farthest star, and what was seen, in involvement, as important is seen, in perspective, as unimportant.

The "mind" expanded to its full measure, especially through listening, embraces all there *is* in immediate awareness.

This limitless "space" in which attention may travel is called Mind as opposed to the "thinking brain" which we generally call "mind".

And to distinguish learning from real knowledge, we shall write the latter as "Knowledge".

*

But where does the control or discipline come from?
Who or what exercises it?
*"Yes," said Sanatkumar. "Will is above mind . . ."*
Whose will?

*

## LISTEN TO THE SILENCE

But there are so many sounds?
What are the sounds contained "in"?
Look at this sentence here on this page
and
Lookatthissentencehereonthispage
Do we only depend on the words for understanding—or also on
the space between each word?

## LISTEN TO THE SILENCE

It contains, surrounds, encompasses every sound.
Reach out to the very farthest sound . . .
What lies beyond it?

## LISTEN TO THE SILENCE

Manas grasps at every passing sound . . .
Buddhi reflects every fleeting desire . . .
I'm not comfortable . . . my cheek itches . . . I want to stop . . .

## LISTEN TO THE SILENCE

What is standing in the way?
Is it not the helter-skelter activity in "mind"?
With Manas pursuing and Buddhi confused?

## LISTEN TO THE SILENCE

Keep attention focused beyond that farthest sound, searching for
the silence.
Is it there?

## LISTEN TO THE SILENCE

and we are taking the first wonderful step in controlling Manas
and Buddhi.
We are, that is, if *now* we are actually going to try the exercise.
It is not at all complicated:
Sit comfortably, close your eyes and then . . .

## LISTEN TO THE SILENCE

*"Is there anything above meditation?"* said Narada.
*"Yes,"* said Sanatkumar. *"Wisdom is above meditation . . ."*

When I begin to explore Mind—and by that is meant the limitless space wherein our total experience of the world takes place, as opposed to the limited, skull-confined "thinking" brain which dreams and schemes—when I begin to explore Mind, at first all that is going on is rather bewildering and elusive.

Compared to my pedestrian dealing with everyday life and problems, the mental processes seem so quick and so subtle.

In fact, we will note that so quickly does the mind act that it is usually only when we stop to look back into our memories that we can recollect what happened.

For example, in conversation, do we not usually speak and reply immediately—on "the spur of the moment"—because the mind has "ready-made" instinctive and habitual ways of responding and reacting? Once established in memory, these response mechanisms operate extremely fast, and we could say that once they are triggered, they act automatically (on our behalf!). Usually the automatic reaction works well enough and we survive each circumstance untroubled; but sometimes we realize afterwards that our reaction has been inappropriate and we regret what we have said or done. Then we say, "If only I had realized . . ." or "I didn't really listen to what was said . . ." or "I didn't really mean what I said . . ." (In itself, this realizing the error, even if only afterwards, may be an important first step, for, if we remember, it can help to avoid repeating the error. It is when we do not even realize a mistake has been made that there is no possibility of becoming wiser!)

*

This may be so.

Is it? I don't know.

I can only find out by observation.

But why is it important? Why should it matter how my mind behaves? Isn't it just as well that it gets on with the job? Ought we to interfere?

Could it not, in fact, be dangerous to get too involved in how mind works!

After all I have heard of people going "out of their minds"—and by that I do not mean "free", I mean "mad".

*

The automatic reaction (re-action; acting again as previously) is due to the mind's conditioning—the accumulation of ideas, beliefs and attitudes that we have adopted and which, impressed in memory, act as a filter for incoming information and then as a pattern or matrix for how we then act or speak.

We may see that, even more deeply or "further back", these ideas, beliefs and attitudes are based on often vague and undefined desires and fears, which may be called the essence of the beliefs we have about ourselves.

For example, one common deep desire could be expressed as "wanting to be liked" (with its counterpart, "fear of being disliked"). How many of our actions are influenced by this one!

Thus, when we speak and act, we are judged "in the sight of others" (judgements which all-too-often reinforce and compound our beliefs about ourselves).

*

But maybe that is how we are?

Why should we attempt to change ourselves?

Is it wise to attempt such a change?

May we not simply be exchanging one set of "automatic re-actions" for another set? Why should the one be preferable to the other?

Whatever we do—we will still be judged "in the sight of others".

*

People will say: "So-and-so is polite . . . rude . . . considerate . . . selfish . . . natural . . . shallow . . . kind-hearted . . . hateful . . . affectionate . . . cold . . . insincere . . . emotional . . ." And so on, and so on.

All these judgements on us are the result of the way in which we have responded to certain situations in the presence of others.

75

According to mood, we may be benign one day and aggressive another, cheerful today, miserable tomorrow. Despite these ups-and-downs, we have, beneath the current mood, established ways of responding and dealing with things and you could say that once they are built in, we seem to be "at their mercy". The deep desires and fears are "unseen", in the dim depths of our consciousness, but continually they colour and influence our response to the world and what it is offering to us.

We tend to overlook the positive and rewarding aspects of our natures and instead harbour and worry about the negative—our shortcomings and failings. In other words, rather than build on our strengths, we tend to concentrate on compensating for our so-called weaknesses. "I wish I were different . . ." or "I wish I was like so-and-so . . ."

Even if we wish we could "change our ways", how often do we actually succeed in doing so? Sometimes circumstances change them for us—as the result of some accident or catastrophe—but that is not through our own volition.

\*

What is volition?
Why is my will weak in some endeavours and strong in others?
How can I be sure that I will change myself for the better?
To what purpose and end should I seek to change myself?
Who would be seeking to change who?
Against what is my will being pitted?

\*

So . . . in beginning to explore Mind and mind, we are discovering a complex, subtle and fast-moving activity, with all kinds of connections, relationships and levels.

Given this situation we will realize that it is no simple matter to "change your mind" *consciously*, knowing who wants to change it, what is to be changed, how it is to be changed and . . . why.

Therefore, let us suggest one important and cardinal "rule":

"I will not endeavour to change anything about myself—until I know what needs to be changed and how and why it needs to be changed . . . and by whose will."

(The reasons for this will, we hope, begin to become apparent.)

*

"But, how can I possibly become wiser . . . nicer . . . better . . . more likeable . . . etc . . . if I don't try to change myself?"

Better, wiser, more likeable . . . in whose eyes?

Other people's?

It is not so simple or straightforward.

Qualities have the characteristic of being "two-faced", according to the circumstances in which they manifest. Someone may say I am easy-going; yet that same quality may be judged by another as being aimless or lazy. One may say I am realistic and objective; another may say disapprovingly of that same quality that I am hard and unsympathetic. One may say I am serious and sincere; another that I have no humour and am tactless.

Two things are becoming clear.

Firstly, there is no way of ensuring the approval of everyone. There is no ideal or perfect person in the eyes of the world. I can spend my life trying to win high esteem but I will never reach the summit because there will always be those who will see shortcomings and limitations.

"All right," I may say, "then let me achieve high esteem in the eyes of those I love and respect." But, supposing I do believe I have managed this, what a problem to stay there—to remain loved and respected. For the object of my attention—the person I seek constantly to impress—is also subject to moods, to change . . . No, as far as the world's assessment is concerned, it is a wild and fruitless chase to try to achieve and maintain an invulnerable state of niceness, goodness, wisdom or whatever.

And secondly, following on from this, it is neither possible nor appropriate to imagine that I can combine and embody all these qualities consistently or permanently. Why? Because they do not exist in themselves; they only manifest in a given moment in a certain circumstance. I cannot have them or summon them . . . or be this or that . . . out of context. It is the context which dictates what needs to be called forth. I may think it is laudable to be judged tolerant; but that judgement will only be appropriate to how I have *once* behaved in a given circumstance. Certainly I may repeat it in another; but it is just as possible that in doing so I will, in the second case, be judged weak-minded.

*

So, how is this resolved?

As suggested, it must be to do with acting appropriately in response to a particular circumstance at a given moment. That circumstance may call from me tolerance—or it may call for deliberate and forceful intervention. In one situation it may be appropriate to be sympathetic; another, apparently similar on the surface, may call for objective criticism or remonstration. In other words, we cannot pre-judge, be prejudiced, about how we ought to behave. The situation dictates—not me.

Of course it is natural to want to be liked, admired, respected . . . but it is quite another matter to *try* to make others like, admire and respect me.

So what is the key?

If the world cannot be relied on to judge me as I want to be judged, who can? (And by the same light, am I justified in judging another?)

*

Is my judgement of myself of any value?

*

Yes!

With certain reservation, and under certain condition, I am the best judge of myself—for in relation to *what* can anyone else judge me?

In relation to religious and social morality and law, I may speak or act immorally or unlawfully, and suffer the appropriate condemnation and punishment. I may be ostracized, incarcerated, have my wealth and possessions taken away from me, be publicly or privately disapproved of by others. In other words, I am punished in the world's ways and terms. But I may be innocent. In the final analysis, only I know, in my heart, whether I am guilty or not. I may actually have committed a crime according to the religious and social code . . . but why did I do it, did I really know it was wrong, could I have stopped myself, what were the perhaps overwhelming circumstances that drove me to it?

Who else can judge the *motives* for my actions but myself?

The world is only really concerned with the *results* of my actions—not with my *motives*, except in so far as the world, by trying to understand motive, may be able to restrain or remove those which give rise to the results which it disapproves of.

Ultimately, deep within, I am the only one who knows my innocence or my guilt. And it is the effect of that which has the far-reaching repercussions for me because, inevitably, I have to live with myself. And I have to discover in what respects my thought, speech and actions benefit or damage me. (This is not to suggest disregard of others—for on how I regard and treat myself will depend how I regard and treat others.)

And how I succeed or fail to "put my own house in order" may have implications far beyond the immediate present. Not only will we discover that it is a lifetime's challenge and endeavour but we may also begin to suspect that it has implications "beyond this life".

*

This introduces us to the Vedic (or Hindu) concept called *karma*.

It is a deep and subtle concept and it has been discussed, argued about, misinterpreted and re-interpreted, many many times over succeeding generations. The confusion and contradiction surrounding it has much to do with the "level of understanding" at which it is being expounded and received.

We cannot do it justice in a brief explanation or definition but it is a bit like the law of physics which states that for every action there will be an equal and opposite reaction. Thus it suggests that to the degree in which we act helpfully or harmfully so we will ourselves he helped or harmed. (In the Bible we could say that St. Paul expressed this principle in saying: ". . . *for whatever a man soweth, that shall he also reap*", and it was suggested by Jesus in saying: "*And as ye would that men should do to you, do ye also to them likewise.*")

But this process is essentially to do with the mind and is very subtle in its working. It does not just mean that if I hit someone, then someone will hit me back, or that if I steal from someone then inevitably I will in turn be robbed (though this should not be entirely discounted as a possibility!). And it does not mean that if I commit a crime against society then I will automatically be punished by society; obviously some people do avoid punishment in that respect and, literally, do "get away with murder".

But what effect the committing of wrong-doing has on the psyche of the perpetrator is quite a different matter. Here, the law is inexorable and inevitable. If I cause suffering, sooner or later I will suffer. This is inescapable, according to the law of karma.

I may regard such a law as preposterous and dismiss it, but . . . let us say that we should not lightly dismiss it for it is highly pertinent to the fulfilment of the three basic desires—for happiness, knowledge and immortality. Hinduism lays great stress on this concept of karma and its realization in practice.

And we should again remind ourselves that it is concerned not just with our actions and their effect but with how I think *before* I act.

*

"As I think, so I am."

*

We will have to observe this law in experience.

It is not difficult to appreciate that how and what we think has considerable effect on our mood or state of mind and hence the quality and kind of our speech and action. It has an effect on what the *Vedas* would call the "mind substance". Negative thinking—selfish, vindictive, bitter, and so on—weakens and "poisons" the psyche; positive thinking—useful, creative, altruistic—"heals", strengthens and enlivens the psyche.

*

In order to focus on what ought to be changed, we could approach the situation this way (and this is only one approach among the many possible):

It seems that when we react "thoughtlessly", it has been because the response has been automatic and immediate, and we have had no chance to control it. Because we are so often not really paying attention—say, because we are thinking about something else or because we are prejudicing the situation, either by "reading" into it something that touches a fear or are trying to mould the situation in pursuit of a selfish desire—we eliminate the chance of seeing the real import and opportunity. We fail to appreciate what is really *needed*.

We could say that it seems to happen so quickly that there is no room between the incoming impressions, then their interpretation, then the deciding what to do about it and then the reaction to it. These phases of the process seem to happen almost instantaneously. It would be useless here to give examples—we must each find them for ourselves. Because, as already stated, we can only each judge ourselves and our behaviour.

In saying that there seems to be no room to interrupt, we are saying that there is not enough *space*—no interstices to get between one phase and the next in the process.

Not enough space.

And how have we suggested that space may be "created"?

By listening.

It is a very strange and "miraculous" experience but if I remember to pay attention and listen, really listen without letting all kinds of prejudicial ideas jump into the mind, then "time slows down" and there is plenty of space to get in between the incoming impression, the interpretation and the decision how to react—and then how I express myself may well be quite different from what it would have been had I been carried away by my immediate reaction.

81

Of course, the immediate reaction may well be natural and appropriate; well and good; I simply let it manifest. On the other hand, if I realize that what I would have said or done would have been harmful, then I have the opportunity to behave more wisely.

Really paying attention (directing Manas) clears the mind (Buddhi) of prejudice and allows space for evaluation which in turn permits appropriate speech and action.

*

But a word of warning before we move on.

Such exercises as this one, where greater control is introduced, inevitably invests the practitioner with power.

And as always with power it can be misdirected and misapplied. It is possible that the greater control may be used to improve the possibility of getting what I want, at the expense of others.

This is why we must remember the cardinal rule—I will not endeavour to change anything about myself—until I know what needs to be changed and how and *why* it needs to be changed . . . and *by whose will.*

*

Another way of putting the need to give space to the mind could be this:

Listening expands the mind (because it is released or liberated from its selfish and subjective concern—its "introspection") and allows it to reach "to the furthest star".

It allows what we call "consideration".

And surely it is not just a coincidence that the word "consideration" means "with the stars" (Latin: con—"with", sideris—"star")!

There is *considerable* significance in this because it implies (in the symbol "star") a level of consciousness and law commensurate with the "heavens", as opposed to the mundane and terrestrial level of scientific fact and learning.

"Worship" of the "heavenly bodies" and the real knowledge of astrology used by the ancient sages reflected a calibre and depth of understanding of Mind which we have almost totally forgotten.

*

## LISTEN TO THE SILENCE

It will become increasingly apparent that these "exercises" should be seriously undertaken by you, the reader (and indeed by us, the writers) for simply to read the words "Listen to the Silence" will make little or no impression on mind. However, if we now actually

## LISTEN TO THE SILENCE

was there not a sensation of the mind being stilled, controlled, disciplined—and at the same time expanding into "space"—reaching out, encompassing time and distance . . .

## LISTEN TO THE SILENCE

*

Now we can move a little closer to the spirit which inspired the Vedic wisdom which still persists amongst the wise, the *gurus,* in the world of Hinduism.

We can perhaps begin to see what they meant by being "liberated"—from the "bondage" of our "closed-circuit" self-concern, a bondage which keeps us well and truly grounded on earth.

By remembering to pay attention and listen, the space is created for consideration.

It makes room for considered response—consideration for the other person, the situation, the environment . . . whatever.

And consideration allows space for Knowledge to enter—the knowing clearly what needs to be said or done in response to need as opposed to what I am tempted to say or do in order to enhance myself, gain for myself, protect myself.

*

And now we must note something absolutely crucial.

All that we have described above about Mind and what goes on in it can only be so described because we are able to observe the experience of it.

*Who is observing it?*

*I am.*

*But who or what is that "I"?*

*Who or what am I?*

Who is listening through my ears, looking through my eyes, observing what is happening in my mind . . . ?

*

"Observe" means "to keep before", in the sense of "holding in front of".

What is the subject "in front of" the object under observation?

*

Is it "me" observing?

Any concept I have about "me" and who I am is *thought* in mind.

Any experience of "me" and mine is experienced in mind.

84

Any idea or belief about "me" is held in what I call my mind and I cannot be aware of having those ideas and beliefs unless I have observed myself to have them.

This at first may seem confusing because usually people think that "I" and "me" are the same thing. But they are not (the former is the subject, the latter an object). We tend to elide the two in our thinking; but it is very important to penetrate, in experience, that the "I" is constant, stable and undefineable; the "me" is continually changing and has all manner of properties.

*

Let me consider, now, everything I think I am.
Everything I think myself to be is thought by me.
And I am aware of everything I think about myself.
Therefore "something" is observing what I am thinking—otherwise I would not be aware of it!

*

The Vedic tradition says that that which is observing all you think you are—and everything else in existence—is the real You, the real "I".
You do not have to believe that as an idea.
*You* can actually experience it to be so.
It is Buddhi, the discriminator or evaluator, which "sees" the difference between the two, and, if it "sees" or reflects clearly, it accepts the distinction as undeniable.
Honestly, then, is that "I" deniable?
And if it is not You, who is it?

*

The Vedic tradition calls the observer of Mind—the ultimate witness of all that there is here and now—*Atman*. And in translation, it is called the Self. In the following quotation, Buddhi is translated as "intellect" and Manas as "discursive mind".

*

85

*"Self rides in the chariot of the body, intellect the firm-footed charioteer, discursive mind the reins.*

*"Senses are the horses, objects of desire the roads. When Self is joined to body, mind, sense, none but He enjoys.*

*"When a man lack steadiness, unable to control his mind, his senses are unmanageable horses.*

*"But if he control his mind, a steady man, they are manageable horses.*

*"The impure, self-willed, unsteady man misses the goal and is born again and again.*

*"The self-controlled, steady, pure man goes to that goal from which he never returns.*

*"He who calls intellect to manage the reins of his mind reaches the end of his journey, finds there all-pervading Spirit.*

*"Above the senses are the objects of desire, above the objects of desire mind, above the mind intellect, above the intellect manifest nature.*

*"Above manifest nature the unmanifest seed, above the unmanifest seed, God. God is the goal; beyond Him nothing."*

(*Katha-Upanishad*)

\*

There are many statements in the Vedic scriptures which help distil an *understanding* of that Self—but no description of the Self itself.

Why?

Because that which witnesses all describable and defineable "things" cannot itself be described or defined. Any description or definition of the Self itself must be the mind's interpretation—and immediately that interpretation is observed by the Self! Hence the Vedic description are of the mind's experience of the presence of the Self.

\*

*The Self is one. Unmoving, it moves faster than the mind. The senses lag . . .*

*. . . is far away, yet near; within all, outside all.*

(*Eesha-Upanishad*)

86

We will gather that the mind has difficulty in conveying experience of the Self. This is because any assertion the mind makes about the Self, the opposite is also true.

The mind—or rather the intellect—ordinarily works through dualities, comparing and measuring one thing against another.

Here, it has to make a kind of quantum jump and see duality as one; it has to comprehend that opposites are two sides of the same thing. The Self is *neti, neti*—"not this, not that".

It is through the necessity for the mind to do this that the Hindu religion or philosophy is able to cope with paradox and apparent contradiction (and why the Western conditioned mind, which likes things to be logical and scientifically provable, baulks at the apparent inconsistency of Hindu thought).

\*

What happens when we remember to *consider*?

We allow space for observation of the situation.

The Self "enters" the space—"I am aware"—and knowledge, if required, advises the mind, permitting objective evaluation and discrimination, resulting in appropriate action.

And what happens to "me" when I really consider the other person, the problem, or the need of the situation?

"Me" disappears.

"Me" is a fiction, an indulgence of the mind, who only appears when the mind is idle or self-concerned—closed and "spaceless".

"Me" has no place in Mind, the expanded space or "consciousness" wherein the Self observes through the senses of the body all there is in the experience of the moment. When "I" am present, "me" is not. In this state, Manas is directed to the need of the moment and Buddhi (synonymous with true intellect—which means something like "picking out among") evaluates and chooses in respect of that need.

\*

"*Self rides in the chariot of the body . . . none but He enjoys.*"

87

"*The seer's duty,*
*Ordained by his nature,*
*Is to be tranquil*
*In mind and in spirit.*
*Self-controlled,*
*Austere and stainless,*
*Upright, forbearing;*
"*To follow wisdom*
*To know the Atman,*
*Firm of faith*
*In the truth that is Brahman.*"
                    (*Bhagavad-Gita*)

We have now introduced a number of ideas and features central to the Vedic tradition, a tradition which in time gave rise to Hinduism (and several other "isms" as well).

As we have said the process of introducing and attempting to explain such ideas in writing is very much limited by the words available and the structure of the language we use. It is a relatively cumbersome, approximate and laboured means of conveying something which is essentially alive, immediate and subtle. It is difficult to describe *experience*.

I may attempt to describe to you the scent of a rose; but how can such a verbal description compare with the actual experience of a rose? If I could give you the rose, you could smell it—and know!

I could write down for you the musical notation to convey to you a song that I love. But unless you can read music and can sing the notes yourself, you will have no experience of the song. If I could sing you the song, you would hear it—and know!

The words have to be translated into personal experience; otherwise our communicating is idle and useless.

The gap between description of experience and actually experiencing is a quantum jump. The theory and the experience belong to different worlds.

Nevertheless, by written word I can direct you to where there is a rose and I can advise you to smell it; by written notation I can convey to you the possibility of hearing my song. It is a start.

*

And this is the essential nature of teaching—leading through knowledge to understanding: it is the vital link between the theory and the experience.

"Drop by drop, the bucket is filled."

What, at first may seem unintelligible—and as we say "beyond me"—can become "learned", and then it is in memory as if we always knew it.

Once, for example, all these L-E-T-T-E-R-S on this page were a meaningless pattern—now they are seen to form "words" which you are reading and which may be understood. Can it be possible that time was, you couldn't read, or I couldn't write? It was another world, another person!

So we have words, with which to communicate.

*

We could say then that words can give direction; but the possibility of that information being translated into experience lies with you alone.

*

But we have not called this book, *The Hindu Word*, nor *The Hindu Thought* nor even *The Hindu Wisdom*—it is, and it can only be, *The Hindu Sound*. We cannot describe a sound to each other. We may try—we may say, "It is a sound rather like this other sound that we both have heard"—but to know the sound for ourselves, we must *hear* it. And here is a rare complexity! You may never know for certain that *I* am hearing the sound in the same way that *you* are. We may stand, side by side, and listen to a single note of music. Yes—we both hear it—but *what* precisely we hear will be for ever, each our own, individual experience.

How exact this is, once we grasp it. A *word* we will both construe, both assess, both understand, but again, individually.

An *idea* we will both consider, both debate, both accept—or reject, independently.

*Wisdom*, we will both evaluate, both discriminate, both merge into . . . each in his own way.

But . . . a single sound . . . will simply and forever be what it does to each of us, individually, in the moment—the NOW—of hearing it.

Is this, therefore, suggesting that we are all doomed to a solitary existence?

But—just for a moment . . . pause and consider:

If you hear a sound and I hear a sound; if we both, for a moment *are* (as suggested earlier) the sound that we each are hearing, then, in that moment, are we not *united*, are we not both joined, as *one in the sound*?

Where is my mind then; where is yours?

Where *my* hearing; where yours?

*

What is the difference between your "I" and my "I"?

*

## ONLY CONNECT

*

*Sound* is the essential unifier, as it were.

We cannot both, actively, taste the same mouthful, nor see the same view (for unless you are seeing through my eyes, your viewpoint must be slightly different), nor feel the same sensation (unless you are able to be *in* my body).

*

## ONLY CONNECT

*

*Sound* connects us—no matter what the sound may appear to be to *me*.

For "sound" is directly linked with the element "space". There can only be "one space"—and we are "in" it.

*

Why should we wish to communicate—to commune, to connect?

Because, in healthy relationships, we are moved to help each other. We both wish to be happy—and naturally we wish to share that happiness, help each other to understand what makes us unhappy. Surely that is our common endeavour? Surely we both wish, with whatever talent and insight we can contribute, to help each other lose our sense of fear, ignorance, loneliness, unhappiness?

*

But it will be to no avail if we just tell each other things!

We have to try to translate the words into experience; we have to make the effort to *understand* each other; only then will we discover that all our disagreement is due to *misunderstanding* each other!

\*

Commonly you and I follow a certain process from the moment we are born.

At birth we are a few pounds or kilos of bone, blood, skin, muscle, nerve, a miraculous, complex and sensitive bundle of bio-chemical systems, with a certain amount of individual characteristic in shape, colour, feature. But we have heads, faces, arms, legs—a common structure—and we both have *life*. And we both continue to have it until we die.

Our first independent and new action in the world is to breathe in air. We remember how to breathe. We breathe separately; and yet we both depend together on air, and will continue to do so until we die.

However, we are not self-sufficient with the life and air we share. We remember how to suck and we feed and drink. And we continue to look for food and drink until we die. Here we appear to separate because it seems that your source of food and drink is not the same as mine. But is that really so? We both depend on the resources of earth to provide for us no matter how divergent the apparent immediate source. Nevertheless we tend to forget this fact and herein lies one of the seeds of our separation and, indirectly, many of our problems. For I learn greed, the taking of more than I need. And in seeking what I think is my requirement, I may deprive you.

\*

In the first years, apart from a certain ability to protest—by crying and agitation of the limbs—we are very much at the mercy of our environment. We have no choice but to live and breathe in the available air and trust that we shall be kept sufficiently warm and provided with adequate and acceptable sustenance.

And we can have no choice in the impressions entering through our senses. What we have mentioned as "mind substance" is at first innocent in that it is susceptible to any arbitrary passing impressions and can do nothing to avoid them. Without ability to reject the discordant and harmful, we have to hope for the best— that the sound, the touch, the sight, the smell will be kind and gentle.

We could say that right from the start the senses are actively receiving impressions. And Manas, the messenger, is active, paying attention to the more dominant impressions and conveying them to mind substance indiscriminately, where they are impressed in the substance, becoming memory. And Buddhi, "primitively" at first, only gradually gains strength from memory, evaluating and discriminating between what is comforting and discomforting the body.

But herein lies the seeds of our future motivation and behaviour— preference for pleasure, avoidance of pain.

*

With a few, rare and momentary exceptions, we were not conscious of this learning and choosing process. We cannot now easily remember those hours and days of our first years—how our basic mind patterns were formed in response to our environment. We had no choice in how our methods and responses were moulded.

Of course I can now surmise that "I was there"—but I did not *know* I was there, at the time.

We could suggest a picture something like this:

ATMAN (Self)
_____

BUDDHI (Evaluating)
....................

MANAS (Carrying attention)
....................

SENSES (Receiving impressions)
....................

THE WORLD

*

The Self is present but "cut off" from the existing being.

What is significant about this state of "innocence" is that because at the time "I was not there" I had no concept of myself as a separate person. I did not *think* of myself as separate from the world—I did not even have a concept of "world"!

I was *one* with the world.

No "me" and "that"—duality.

*It was*—or rather, at the time, *It is*.

*

Then I begin to learn *about* the world.

Apart from learning in relation to the sensations and feelings in my body—what was pleasurable and what was painful—I began to pick out "sound-forms", names, and, associating them with images, I remembered them.

Some names, the "good" ones, were associated with pleasant memories; some, the "bad" ones, were associated with unpleasant memories. And thus I began to respond according to that learning, welcoming the good and protesting and protecting against the bad. And therein lay the seed of prejudice, for I assumed that certain images would repeatedly provide the agreeable and others would again repeat the disagreeable.

So, my emerging intellect—Buddhi—grew in strength and, naturally, devoted itself to discriminating between pleasure and pain, aided by memory which was being increasingly impressed with learning the sources of both.

*

And, called by a certain name (my name), memory learned to associate the experience of this body-image with the concept "me"

Things could now be thought of as happening to "me".

And thus arose the belief in "me" being separate from "my" environment.

The experience "it is" became "me" and "that".

*

94

The ability to draw upon the learning of memory gave rise to what later would become the concept "past". What had been learned had already happened. At first it was simply a case of relating the present experience with learning stored in memory.

But such is the special capacity of man, there arose then the ability to "imagine"—the power of imagination—which is the ability to project into the future. The capacity to do this is frequently applied to the projection of a sequence of events based on past learning. It became possible to envisage the repetition of the past.

So, for "me", time was created.

As a baby I had had no concept of passing time. But now I had learned about past, present and future.

*

Imagination is an extraordinary and powerful capacity in man, with enormous ramifications, both for his downfall and the fulfilment of his destiny. The ability to imagine the future is the basis of both fear and hope.

In its first appearance, there is the tendency to relegate it very firmly to the service of pleasure-seeking and pain-avoidance.

There is nothing wrong in that—he would be a fool who deliberately reversed the natural preference. The reservation is the degree to which he might pursue the pleasant and seek to avoid the pain, regardless of the consequences to himself or anyone else.

In this ability to anticipate reward and punishment lies the seed of prejudice, the temptation to pre-judge people and events, an exaggerated and desperate self-concern.

So involved does man tend to become with projecting the learning of the past into an imagined future that he becomes increasingly oblivious of opportunity in the present ("that which is given now").

But the point of all this is that it is in this process that "me"— the supposed person of the past and the imagined person of the future—is created and developed in mind.

*

The above is a crude and approximate model, but in whatever

way it is analysed and expressed, the bare bones of it can be verified in the remembered experience of each one who cares to trace back what happened in his early life—how we each of us have come to think we know who we are. One may describe it differently from another and may dispute the use of certain words but it is the gist of a process common to all men born into this world.

In traditional Far Eastern terms (Vedic, Buddhist, Hindu or whatever) the process is described, in so many words, as "the turning outwards—of Buddhi—to the senses", a movement in which the Self becomes involved in "the illusion of reality" or hidden in "the sheaths of ignorance".

*

In the Katha-Upanishad, Wajashrawas, wanting heaven, gave away all his property. His son, Nachiketas, asked Wajashrawas to whom *he* had been given . . .

"*He went to his father and said: 'Father, have you given me to somebody?' He repeated the question a second and a third time; at last his father said: 'I give you to Death.'*"

The *Upanishad* continues as a dialogue between Nachiketas and Death.

. . . *Death said: 'God made sense turn outward, man therefore looks outward, not into himself. Now and again a daring soul, desiring immortality, has looked back and found himself.*

'*The ignorant man runs after pleasure, sinks into the entanglements of death; but the wise man, seeking the undying, does not run among things that die.*

'*He through whom we see, taste, smell, feel, hear, enjoy, knows everything. He is that Self.*

'*The wise man by meditating upon the self-dependent, all-pervading Self, understands waking and sleeping and goes beyond sorrow.*'

*

So what has happened to the Self in the process?
Where do "I" come into all this?

*

"I", the Self, enters mind with the first thing consciously remembered. ("Consciousness" is said to be one of the three "qualities" of Self—the other two being "Knowledge" and "Bliss").

We could say that the Self is consciously present in the experience of "Self-consciousness" (and it is what the Christian would call "entry of the Holy Spirit").

*

Look at a photograph of yourself as a young child—one that evokes a memory of the situation when the photograph was taken.

You may be told, "This is you when you were . . . years old."

You look at a stranger?

In no way would you know that that image was anything to do with "you"—if you hadn't been told so. It could be the photograph of any child—and it is quite possible that you would prefer not to have to believe it was "you"!

The mental effort required to equate and relate that "you then" with "you now" produces a strange feeling? As though it is a false and illusory make-believe?

And yet—you remember that lawn, that distant view, the heat of that summer's afternoon, the colour of that bicycle, the tear in that doll's dress? Yes . . . I must have been there, looking through that child's eyes, feeling through that child's skin, responding to that experience at that moment.

Yes . . . *You* were there at the moment of remembering the impressions.

The body-image in that photograph is not and was not You—but You were there experiencing *through* that body.

And it is not the same body you are experiencing *through* today—as You look through your eyes at these words.

Are You the body? Or are You that which is experiencing *through* the body?

*

Moments or flashes of self-consciousness happen now and again early in life.

D

97

But they tend to happen more frequently and forcefully at the time of puberty—coincidentally with the emergence of sexual power. (And in the Hindu tradition the two factors are recognized as inter-related.) Such impulses disturb the closed-circuit thinking of self-concern and questions arise in the mind. Above all, questions that are deep, searching and related to wanting to know the reality— "Who am I?"

\*

We are told—and we assume—that we "grew up".

And we tend to assume, due to our having believed in past and future time, that this was a continuous process—that we were born in 19?? and having continued for ?? years that we are now ?? years old.

Yet, looking back and recalling from memory, does it honestly seem like that?

Or is it more like a series of discreet, disconnected moments remembered, which the mind then orders into a logical, worked-out sequence?

It is really quite simple—the moments remembered were "when You were there". The long, forgotten gaps were when the mind was not conscious of Your presence.

\*

## LISTEN
## LISTEN TOWARDS
## LISTEN TOWARDS SILENCE
## NOW

In all the activity going on in mind (and it is said that an idea or thought-impulse comes in every third of a second!) *is* there silence? Does it not seem apparent that the more we seek SILENCE the more irritatingly *busy* mind becomes.

If only we could listen to some *thing*.

Then we could attend?

All right: the process has not been wasted.

We may have learned that mind is never still—while we are "awake".

What can we listen to?

A sound?—certainly.

Or the sound of a thought? One thought. Only one. What thought? Let us select one—and every time mind moves away from it to other thoughts, and we *notice* that this has happened, (who notices?) let us return to the thought.

What thought? Let me be very precise and basic. Let me

## LISTEN TO A QUESTION

But let me be sure of what I am doing.

I will *listen to a question*—not seeking an *answer* just listening to the *question*.

Mind will want to answer: turn back to the question.

Mind will find it "boring". (It could be just that! It could bore its way through mind!)

Listen to a question.

Any question? Well obviously the more powerful the question— the more powerful the exercise.

What is my most pressing and deepest question?

## LISTEN
*Who am I?*

So, to continue a little further with the "growing up".

At a certain stage in the development of you as an individual—the physical organism with its attendant mind activity—there is a directing of attention to the enjoyment of pleasure and the avoidance of discomfort and pain. (In this endeavour we can see reflections of the three principal desires—for happiness, knowledge and immortality.) And then, beyond that rather passive acceptance of what happens to you, there develops the imagination and the ability to project into the future. This provides more active endeavour and motivation—to *pursue* possible pleasure and to *escape* the presumed threat of discomfort and pain. In other words, behaviour is directed towards achieving certain results for myself, and I begin to believe I have *will* and *choice*.

And with the capacity to will (synonymous with "will" as determination of the future: "I will say this . . . or I will do that") came the temptation to concentrate on my own interests, regardless of the expense incurred and heedless of the consequences.

*

And this is how "me" is created.

Something is happening.

There is the thought, automatic and instantaneous, "It is happening to *me*!"

"Do I like it? Yes; then let it continue . . . and how can I improve, intensify, prolong the pleasure . . . Or, no, I do not like it . . . then how can I stop, divert, avoid its continuation?"

With the entry of self-consciousness, I, the Self, enters mind and creates and believes in "me". "Me" takes the Self in vain.

So, if we remember to observe, we will realize that "me" is just a label, an invention in the mind based on the body-image. "Me" is a physical location in time and space with an attendant intelligence directing its activity.

As a word, "me" serves its purpose in the moment—"You tell me" or "You give me" tells you in which direction to speak or offer your gift.

Otherwise "me" is a fictional, transitory creature of the mind—

who is imagined as "having been" in the past or who "will" undertake certain actions in the future.

Ask yourself, now, "What is me?"

Give full attention to that question.

The answer? *I* do not know.

For, as far as *I am* concerned, in the moment of giving attention to that question—or in any present moment of giving attention to all that *is* here and now—there is no "me"!

What a strange game we play!

When *I* (the nominative, the real Self) am present, me (the object, the accusative,) *is not*.

Here lies the crux of the Vedic teaching. For the degree to which I creates and believes in me, so the Self is bound—in the "bondage of the flesh". And to the degree in which I cease to believe in the transitory and inconstant me, so I, the Self, is liberated.

*

The baby has no conception of himself or herself as a separate entity, separate from his or her environment.

"It is as it is."

Only at the entry of the Spirit, the Atman, as Consciousness in the mind, is there the experience of self-consciousness. And immediately, the Atman associates and identifies with the body.

"I am" becomes "I am this or that."

And immediately, this "me" is separated, appears distinct from, the "world about me".

In the process, (in Christian terms, "the fall") I am forgotten. Buddhi "turns outwards" and the mind becomes almost totally concerned with keeping track of "me", the body-associated fiction, who wills pursuit of pleasure and avoidance of pain.

Again, we should remind ourselves, there is nothing "wrong" with this process. It is inevitable. It is "natural" and the way in which we take our places and play our parts in the world. It is as it is Willed and Designed. For it has Purpose. It is because of this very fall into illusion that man is enabled to "climb back" and realize the Truth.

*

So, we have arrived at a point where we can comprehend two possibilities, and it is to the recognition of these two possibilities and their distinction that the Vedic teaching is primarily directed as, in varying terminology, is every other religion in its true sense.

The Vedic tradition however, has a complete "dictionary" of the terms necessary to specify every nuance of mind concept and process.

To structure and distinguish the two possibilities, we can make use of the terms we have now introduced (though, of course, it is a simplified and incomplete view with many subtle qualifications).

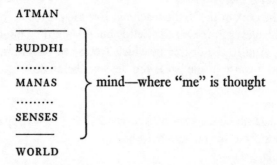

In this situation, we have the self-concerned, self-interested, "small-minded" belief in "me" and "the world out there"—the Self identified with the body-image in a state of "ignorance", "delusion", "bondage"—which can only terminate in "the death of me".

As distinct from:

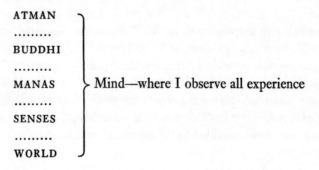

In this situation, we have the evolved, expanded awareness, attention-paying, outward concern of non-identified freedom. In this state lies the possibility of meeting need, realizing the Truth, "liberation" and the key to understanding "immortality".

If we begin to *sense* (hear, touch, see, taste and smell) the distinction between these two—and the distinguishing of them must be a matter of experience, of observation, for there is no value in the theory of it—we have to emphasize one principle.

It is not possible for them to exist simultaneously.

Each is only known in contrast with the other—there has to be the fall from innocence into the first state and then an "awakening" to the second state for the distinction to be known or *realized*.

The process has to follow the sequence—innocence, ignorance, remembering. (We could call it—not knowing "God", ignoring or forgetting "God", remembering or knowing "God".)

\*

I
I am I
I forget I am I
I believe me is I
I wonder, who am I?
I do not know that I am I
I realize me is not I
I must be I
I am I
I

\*

Why should one state be preferable to the other?

This is a preference that Buddhi, the discriminator, has to make when presented with the evidence. It depends on the experience of the individual and the degree of "longing in the heart for Truth". Accordingly, choice is made and, relatively speaking, it is fundamentally ("in the depths of the mind") the only *real* and *conscious* choice the individual has.

As an individual person, you can continue to maintain the beliefs you have about yourself, your image in the eyes of the world, your belief in what you vaguely think you are, your idea that you are some kind of permanent and consistent entity separate from the world . . . or there can be surrender of all that as being commitment to illusion.

(And here we have a parallel with Christian self-sacrifice—as dramatically enacted, at a "higher" level, in the symbolic Jesus surrendering to his crucifixion. We would call it "higher" level because the "voluntary suicide" of that ultimate crucifixion signifies a "surrender of my life" for which the surrender we are talking about is a preliminary preparation.)

Buddhi, then, either serves "me" in my assumed status in the world . . . or it serves "I" in response *to* the world.

*

And this is where we can refer back to our cardinal rule: "I will not endeavour to change anything about myself, until I know what needs to be changed, and how and why it needs to be changed, and by whose will."

The difficulty is that in believing I ought to change myself I am only saying "me wants to improve me". It is a bit like "trying to lift yourself by your own boot laces"! I may be able to improve myself temporarily in certain respects, in certain circumstances . . . but the trouble is the circumstances change and my improvement wavers and wanes. I do not seem to be able to find an absolute standard to measure myself by. And, further, I cannot see the ultimate purpose in the service of which I am attempting to perfect myself.

On the other hand, supposing I surrender all preconception as to how I should behave in my own estimation? Supposing by paying full attention to the circumstances, I could trust that I will respond appropriately to the *need* of the situation at that moment. For sure, I could be certain that my behaviour will not be motivated by self-concern!

Under such a discipline, the behaviour would be changed according to the need, and not according to my will.

I do not change anything according to my ideas as to how they should be changed . . . but the behaviour changes "of itself", in response to the requirement "outside myself".

By whose Will will it then be done?

*

"*Diverging roads; one called ignorance, the other wisdom. Rejecting images of pleasure, Nachiketas! you turn towards wisdom.*

"*Fools brag of their knowledge; proud, ignorant, dissolving, blind led by the blind, staggering to and fro.*

"*What can the money-maddened simpleton know of the future? 'This is the only world' cries he; because he thinks there is no other I kill him again and again.*

"*Some have never heard of the Self, some have heard but cannot find Him. Who finds Him is a world's wonder, who expounds Him is a world's wonder, who inherits Him from his Master is a world's wonder.*

"*No man of common mind can teach Him; such men dispute one against another. But when the uncommon man speaks, dispute is over. Because the Self is a fine substance. He slips from the mind and deludes imagination.*

"*Beloved! Logic brings no man to the Self. Yet when a wise man shows Him, He is found . . .*"

(Katha-Upanishad)

Whose will is writing this book?
The writers ask themselves this question over and over again.
*Whose will is writing this book?*

Why do we choose to write it?
Because we are being rewarded to write it?
Because we think we know?
Because we seek to discover?
Because we yearn for the Self?

Is the book a mutual exploration into the labyrinthine wisdom of the Vedas?
A seeking to discover that which is already Knowledge in Mind but is forgotten in mind?
Is the book an attempt, through experience, actually to strip away the many sheaths of illusion and to reveal, make real, that I AM?
*Why are we writing this book?*
*Why?*

\*

This isn't some sort of an inter-office memo between the two authors, which the reader would be advised to skip!
Far from it.
"The authors"—we, the writers—have, during the work on this book, been experiencing the true working of the Vedanta.
It is not without pain.
Let that be a warning. If you want to pursue the path of Truth— it will not be without pain. But the "pain" also is an illusion . . . and is balanced by the continuing joy of discovery and a greater freedom.

It all depends upon what the individual wants—a life of half-truths, or the full glory of the Truth? Darkness or light?

It takes effort to climb to the top of a mountain, but, once there, the view can be rewarding.

*

So far this book may seem to have been a series of ideas, theories and many, many words.

Some people will perhaps have responded to them—others may have given up. (We will come to the different types of people in more detail later.)

But you—who are now reading the words—if the words are not "working in you" they are meaningless: for "a word means what it *does*."

And meaningless words very soon become irritating! We each have more than enough buzzing in mind without adding to the store with someone else's out-pourings of mind!

Can we even be sure that the Vedanta was ever more than that? The busy out-pourings of someone else's mind?

We—the authors—are suggesting that *The Hindu Sound* was the expressing, in everyday terms, of the Truth; and that that expressing came through the Wise and is contained in Mind.

But why should you take our word for it?

Clearly, there is no reason at all why you should consider this book as anything more than just a book. A book "about" . . .

A book "about" an ancient civilization and the way it thought . . .

*

Does it seem distant and far away? What, you may ask—as I, the writer, ask—has it got to do with *me*?

The history of the Hindu religion may be found in countless books. Go to any library and look along the shelves . . .

The Vedic "scriptures"—the *Upanishads*, the *Bhagavad-Gita*, *Vivekachudamani*—may be read, albeit in translation from the Sanskrit, anytime, anywhere. Get copies and you may read them . . .

*

But it will all still be "out there". History from the past, words on a page, theories in my mind . . .

Will it ever, can it ever, *change me*?

Can the ancient writings from an even more ancient civilization change me *now*? help me *now*? liberate me *now*?

If I am looking for a faith to cling on to in this life—will I find it in the Vedanta?

If I am looking for an ideal-being (a Jesus, a Buddha, a Mohammed . . . ) to aspire to, to shape my life, to strive to imitate—will I find such a being? Where is the leader who spoke the words of the Vedas?

If, in short, I am looking for a god to worship and adore, who may give me hard laws to obey, who may lift me up when I am "good" and cast me down when I am "bad" . . .

"Where is God in the Vedas?" I cry out.

What has the Vedanta to do with *me*?

\*

## EXPERIENCE
## OBSERVATION
## DISCRIMINATION

\*

Every single *experience* that you have—that I have—is the "scripture" of the Vedas. (Remember, there was a time when they were not written down—when they were songs.) Every song is the expression of experience and every experience, a song.

Every moment of the day—*now*, as I write these words, *now*, as you read them—there is *experiencing* going on.

*Now* there is *experience*.

*Now* is the scripture of the Vedas.

\*

Every time that you *observe*, that I *observe*, the experience, that is the "faith" of the Vedas. Usually we experience, and only recall the experience in retrospect. Things happen and later, even months later, we note that they have happened. But *observation* is watching *as the experience is taking place*.

*Now*, as you read these words, *observe*. Not the words on the page, deeper than that.

*Now*, at this moment, ask yourself: "Who is looking through my eyes?"

Such *observation* will reveal (make real) that I AM. For it isn't "me" that observes—is it?

＊

Every time that you *discriminate*, that I *discriminate*; every time that we ask ourselves "Who is *observing* the *experience*?" then the questioner, the observer, the experiencer through discrimination, is the "ideal-being" of the Vedas.

Who needs a being to imitate—when each being contains the Self?

＊

The Vedic tradition may be an ancient system of philosophy—but it was speaking directly to people like you, like me, who were desirous of finding Knowledge, the "seekers after Truth". If anyone *now* reading this book is also desirous of Knowledge, then the Vedanta is as alive today as it ever was. For its words mean what they do—to you—to me.

We are not asked to *believe* anything . . .

EXPERIENCE
OBSERVATION
DISCRIMINATION

# LISTEN
## LISTEN TO NEAR SOUNDS

your breathing, salivations in the mouth, your heart beating, your pulse, your clothing rubbing against your skin.
Sounds "outside" you, sounds "inside" you.

# LISTEN
## LISTEN TO MORE DISTANT SOUNDS

The sounds in the room, the sounds in the street outside the room, the sounds beyond those sounds, the sound beyond . . . even further.
As far as it is possible, send out your listening . . .

# NOW

with the mind still—turn your attention that has been focused on those more distant sounds.
*Turn your attention right round—180 degrees.*

# NOW
## LISTEN TO YOUR INNER-MOST POINT

as you sought the distant sounds outside—seek now the deepest point within.
Try it!
Try it every day.
You may think that you are falling asleep doing this exercise.
But what does that mean? *Who* fell . . . *where?*
Try it now—just for a few moments . . .
Start by listening outwards—then, turn the attention and listen deep within.
It is the beginning of an exercise that can take us "all the way".
Yes, there is more to it than this. But let us start from here.
Try it.

# NOW

*So, with his heart serene and fearless,*
*Firm in the vow of renunciation,*
*Holding the mind from its restless roaming,*
*Now let him struggle to reach my oneness,*
*Ever-absorbed, his eyes on me always,*
*His prize, his purpose . . .*
                              *(Bhagavad-Gita)*

" . . . but the trouble is the circumstances change and my improvement wavers and wanes. I do not seem to find an absolute standard to measure myself by. And, further, I cannot see the ultimate purpose in the service of which I am attempting to perfect myself . . ."

That statement, in so many words, states the human predicament. Many will recognize it and find it echoing in the depths of the mind. Many will not admit it because they have never been moved to consider such thoughts. Many will have touched such an admission and will have pushed it fearfully aside, ignored it, covered it up—and pressed on with the immediate business of surviving today and imagining tomorrow.

The "Western" mind tends to be inculcated with the belief that man by his own will can perfect himself, create the Utopian ideal and eventually live in peace and plenty for evermore. Unfortunately, such a goal is dependent on everyone aiming for the same defined ideal and history suggests that, for all the scientific and technological advance, this fulfilment is proving ever-elusive and the momentum towards it is only maintained by vague and desperate hope. Anyone who cares to ponder on the centuries of painful human experience must surely admit that the Western philosophies of material growth show very little promise of providing peace and plenty for everyone. "That is defeatist!" comes the protest. Is it? Might that not be the cry of one who dare not admit that he is committed to a philosophy which he must pursue because he cannot see an alternative?

Yes, we will say; man may be able to achieve the ideal on earth through the use of will, wit and intelligence . . . if he will only comprehend "whose" Will, Wit and Intelligence it really is.

At the same time, it must be said that the "Eastern" mind, inculcated with modern interpretation (and by "modern" is meant a period covering the past two thousand years) of the Vedic philosophy has tended to move towards the opposite pole—surrender of will, responsibility and endeavour. This has tended to produce a fatalism and apathy which results in aimlessness, poverty and chaos.

The effect is a kind of mirror-image of the "Western" situation because the mistake is the same. As opposed to confidence in "self-will" we have surrender of "self-will"; and the mistake in both cases is failure to comprehend the source of Will. We may begin to see that it is appropriate and wise to surrender self-will . . . but only if it is in acknowledgement of "higher" Will. Surrender of self-will does not mean passive apathy; rather active participation in response to need.

These are broad generalizations but, fundamentally, they indicate a quality that each can recognize in himself as well as in the world at large. It is as if the two halves, "East" and "West", are represented in each one of us—the passive and the active, the contemplative and the doer of deeds (or the idle and the overactive).

Once again we see dichotomy in man—in the individual and in mankind as a whole. And it is not a case of one being preferable to the other. It is not a case of westernizing the "East" or easternizing the "West". Each can throw light on the other, contribute to the other, each reducing the excessiveness and exaggeration of the other. As with male and female, they are equal but not the same; one should not oppose the other but complement it.

But this does not take place of itself. The duality has to be resolved through a third, conditioning factor. By our own self-will we shall not find the balance between active and passive. Only through surrender to "higher" Will will we find the natural rhythm between passive contemplation and active participation and thus eliminate our excesses of idleness and interference.

*

But now to return to our immediate and personal quest.

We go about our daily business. Events have led us to where we are—and we cannot, seemingly, change our history. Each of us has apparently had no say in what is happening to us today, nor how adequately we may be equipped to deal with what may happen in an hour's time, tomorrow, next week, next year. We hope for the best.

(For as the *Chhandogya-Upanishad* asserts, hope is second only to life itself. Without hope for a "bettering", there is not much left except blind assumption that we may at least continue.)

"Will" may simply reside in the fact that given the opportunity I "will" fulfil my dream tomorrow; and choice may reside in the belief that confronted with alternatives I "will" be wise enough to choose the one most likely to expedite my dream; and "wisdom" itself may reside in the assumption that if I learn not to repeat past mistakes I will not obstruct the realization of that dream.

The idle mind—the mind not at present directed to a particular task—"enjoys" itself imagining blissful possibilities or "frightens" itself imagining the repetition of past nightmares. Such dreams leave their imprint and influence our behaviour, continually luring and exciting the mind, distracting it from the reality of the moment.

Again, this is what the Vedic tradition calls involvement in "the sheaths of illusion" which veil the Reality.

But if I remember, am aware of, this moment now, I can resist the pressure of my desire and the panic of my fear and give attention to what is actually happening and respond to what it is actually offering.

Opportunity is always here and now.

Only *now* can I become wiser by ceasing to repeat past mistakes. Only *now* can my karma be redeemed (for the Vedas say that karma holds *me* on the "wheel of continuing rebirth", a repetition of suffering again and again). Only *now* can I respond to what is required *of* me, instead of pursuing what "me" thinks it wants.

Will is done when I am conscious *now*.

When I will, it is done.

Will is present in self-will . . . but the outcome is quite different. It is then done *in spite of me*.

I, me; subject, object; nominative, accusative.

And in between? The vocative, the calling voice, the sound of the name—"Thou".

The Vedas speak and say, "*Tat Tvam Asi*"—"Thou art that".

(As the Christian says, "Thy will be done".)

But who art Thou?

The mind wishes to know.

I am.

*

I

A letter, a number, a symbol.

A letter, an upright line, standing for the sound of a name (nominative). A sound uttered as statement to signify this "being" here; this person ("through sound") present (approximately "before being here"); this individual ("not divisible", "not seeing two.")

A number signifying one, single, alone, not-two, standing for the whole, *the* existing entity (as opposed to the not-existing no-thing). It is a statement of the All—because if there were another, a second, then there would not be one.

We speak of *a* person (indefinite) but not of an "I". It is *the* "I" (definite).

A symbol, written and spoken, which we do well to consider and contemplate.

*

As *The* Principal it stands—I.
From it stems this person—this person now reading these words.
It is the principal on which depend all persons.
All persons depend on I.
In the Vedic tradition this principal is called Atman—the Self.
We are all enlivened by the I. "I will . . . "
Under that principal we are all joined as one.
I enters—as Spirit—into Matter to give "being" or "consciousness" to Mind-substance.

And the Mind-substance enlivened expresses the experience with the sound "I am".

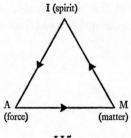

I (spirit)

A                    M
(force)            (matter)

And the mind, in acknowledgement of that which enlivens it, responds in praise, "Thou art".

And in doing so realizes (makes real) "It is".

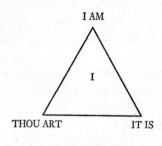

*

I am.
We are.
All is.
On behalf of the seas, the mountains, the trees, the flowers, the animals, the birds, the cloud, the storm, the earthquake—the human voice sings, "I am, Thou art, It is."

*

Of course, we are playing with words. (What else, we may ask, should we be doing with them?)

But, in the play, the mind—or rather Buddhi, the intellect—reflects the sounds and their patterns and Manas searches the experience stored in memory and there is response ("pledging oneself again", "answering oneself" or, we could say, "answering the One Self").

Yes, it is Known what the words, the sounds, are meaning; there is Knowledge of what the sounds are *doing*. They are calling, invoking the Spirit, recalling the Being from the Mind-substance.

I *know* I am.

*

Yes, it is just an explanation.
But "just" is just—precise, lawful.

"Explanation" means "out of the plane", out of the two-dimensional, flat world of competing dualities and opposites.

Explanation can lift understanding into a third dimension—a "higher level" of consciousness.

*

I.

I am.

I know I am—Self-conscious.

That is how it is for man—as distinct from the wind, the birds, the grass and the lightning.

I am created, born of Spirit and Matter, the real "father" and "mother" of man, who may realize himself to be the "son".

*

We have spoken of the simple, singular and total—I am.

But it is not enough just to be here!

Man is a particular creature and as an incarnate, particular mammal has to function in the physical world. He must breathe, eat, drink and participate in the survival of the species.

And in becoming involved in that function, Buddhi "turns outwards towards the senses", ignoring the I principal, forgetting I am, and deals with the plurality, the multitude of things (the "we are", the "you are" and the "they are"). And the imagination, creating time, casts the plurality into the past (the "have been") and projects them into the future (the "will be", the "could be" and the "ought to be").

The force of impulse or "creation" makes all manner of things to appear and mind separates them all.

"I am" becomes "I am something".

And "I" believe that "I am this, that or the other".

"Believing"—I "lease my being to it". I give it credence.

*

In the maturing child, who does not consciously *know* "I am" except in rare moments, the Self identifies with the senses and comes to associate with the body.

117

He or she learns to believe "I am this body".

And from that fundamental identification ("the making of an entity out of the 'id'—the 'that' ") hangs all that follows:

I am hungry; I am thirsty.

I am big; I am small.

I am strong; I am weak.

I am beautiful; I am ugly.

I am different; I am separate . . .

And the more the child, and later the adult, learns, the stronger the identification and the more the involvement is compounded, especially as there is increasing comparison, contrast and competition of "me" with another . . .

I am well; I am ill.

I am successful; I am a failure.

I am a winner; I am a loser.

I am clever; I am stupid.

I am happy; I am sad.

I am a believer; I am an atheist.

I am a Hindu; I am a Christian . . .

A thousand, thousand things I become and believe "I am".

I could fill this book with what I think I am.

(And I could fill another book with what I think others are.)

And, in memory, these are all the things I have become—"*come to be*".

*

Are these things that I think I am, truly what I am?

How do I come to be these things?

Because, having entertained the idea as a thought, I believed—I "leased my being" to it.

Why I believed and continue to believe certain things about myself (and why you do!) and why I refused to believe other things about myself need not concern us here. (It has to do with the concept we have mentioned, karma, and coming to understand later in development exactly what a particular person's role in his or her life should be.) It is sufficient that we concentrate on this phenomenon "believing".

For once I have believed I must inevitably bear and cope with the consequences of that belief—for as long as I choose to hold it.

*

The power of belief resides in the fact that once a belief is adopted and maintained, Buddhi "sees" it as "truth".

"I am hungry . . . Of course I am hungry! That is undeniably true!"

"I am ill . . . Of course I am ill! That is undeniably true!"

And yet . . . is it not the *body* that is hungry or ill?

*

And memory enhances and reinforces the power of belief.

"I am happy . . . Of course I am happy! . . . I know I am happy today because I was unhappy yesterday. That is undeniably true!"

And yet, if we look carefully, we will see that what I ought to be saying, a little more truthfully, is "I am *happier* today than I was yesterday". The condition is relative.

And is there such a thing as absolute happiness?

It may be *relatively* true to say I am more happy than I was yesterday, last year, when I was young . . . but it would not be *the* truth to say "I am happy" unless I knew the complete, unassailable, permanent state of happiness (what the translators of the Vedas call "absolute bliss").

And herein lies the trap or the illusion. For while it may be harmless and enjoyable to be able to say today "I am happy", unless I really understand the nature of happiness and what it depends upon, I leave myself wide open to believing tomorrow that "I am unhappy."

What does happiness depend upon?

Everything going "right" for *me*?

If so, then I must accept the consequences of everything going "wrong" for me also.

*

And the powers of comparison and imagination reinforce my belief.

"I am a failure . . . Of course I am a failure . . . Because someone else is successful in the same endeavour . . . Or because I have not achieved the result that I imagined I could. That is undeniably true!"

And yet, again, is there a complete, unassailable, permanent success? In what accomplishment has a man ever been absolutely successful?

All succeeding and failing is relative—related in the worldly sense to imagined and vague superlatives.

For in relation to what do I think I can measure my success or failure?

It may be "true" that I am wealthier, more powerful, more famous, more learned than someone else. But in believing that, I leave myself wide open to being poorer, less powerful, less famous, less learned than another someone else.

And if I become the wealthiest, the most powerful, most famous and most learned person on earth, what will it avail me?

For again, my success or failure must always remain temporary, relative and mundane.

Of course it is natural and appropriate that I should wish to "better" myself—but the trap or illusion resides in the directions in which I believe I can do so.

\*

What I think I am or may become—or rather what "me" is or might be—is always relative to disconcertingly elusive and impermanent criteria—in the world's terms.

To experience happiness is pleasant and I am grateful for the fleeting moments when I can say "I am happy." But how many will there be and will I ever be able to hold on to one permanently?

To have achieved success is rewarding and I am proud occasionally to be able to say "I am successful." But how permanent is the success? Will I ever be able to rest in the certain knowledge that I have achieved absolute success?

To have status in the world is reassuring and I may be able to take satisfaction from the fact that "I am a shop-keeper" or "I am a doctor" or "I am a prime minister." But what am I when I retire? An "ex-shop-keeper", an "ex-doctor", an "ex-prime-minister?" A "has been?" Nothing?

To cry triumphantly, "I am alive!" may be an expression of present exultation . . . but if only that did not mean that one day "I shall be dead."

*

And here we begin to see the double-edged outcome of man's capacity to compare with the past and imagine the future.

A dog may be evidently content or manifestly ill—it shows it in every fibre of its being. But does it fear distress tomorrow or hope for the return of health next week?

Whether it does or not, for sure it is man's capacity to compare and imagine that plays havoc with the security of the beliefs that he attempts to maintain.

For the memory of past misery can make him fearful for the continuation of present happiness.

And the memory of successes faded can make him wary of present achievement.

And the memory of loved ones wrested from him by death can fill his present love with poignancy, and make him wonder as to the purpose of all his endeavour in that death is the very antithesis of permanency in anything.

Because he senses the relativity of the present happiness or learning, it is almost in perverse desperation that he is willing to believe— put his trust in—a better tomorrow. It is desperate because he is willing to do so in spite of the evidence in memory that no today has ever provided the lasting happiness and certain wisdom longed for yesterday. And desperate because in banking on tomorrow, he tends to overlook the opportunity of the present moment. For happiness and wisdom manifest here and now—or not at all.

So what is to be said in favour of this capacity to remember the past and imagine the future?

Perhaps the very fact that they *can* play havoc with the security of his belief?

It is the very fact, perhaps, that they demonstrate to him that there is no firm foundation in the ideas and ideals of human invention. Having once realized that, then he may turn away from putting his trust in them. And begin to search for what he may truly trust.

As the Vedas would say, he begins to remove the sheaths of illusion.

And the Vedas reassure us that we do not have to search for "Truth", "God", "happiness", "wisdom" or whatever. It is sufficient that we desist from believing in what we discover to be illusion or untruth. For the degree to which we cease to believe the untruth, so the Truth becomes apparent *of Itself*.

\*

When I have projected what I think I am into what I hope I will be, I have reached the end of the line, the end of the creative impulse. Beyond that, there is no further to go. My hope and endeavour is in a *cul-de-sac*.

(And if by chance the emphasis is not on hope for the future but fear and pessimism, then that is real desperation, for without hope, there is no alternative but the "escape" of self-destruction.)

So what must I do if I realize that it is a *cul-de-sac*?

Turn round.

And having turned round, what then?

Start to go back.

I start to undo and disentangle myself from what I perceive has been commitment to false belief.

\*

Let us now consider this book.

We, the writers, have attempted to give an indication of the Vedantic tradition—its structure and its approach to certain basic questions, common to all people.

We have now come to a point along the way.

(In other words, there is more structuring, more concept still to be introduced.)

However, some of us may now be finding that we cannot take too much more of this strange and possibly mystifying philosophical system. In the end, if such a system does not become part of me, if it is not recognizable to me as being to do with me—then it will never be more than a quaint set of teachings and beliefs belonging to other men.

Thus we may see pictures of other tribes performing strange ritualistic dances, we may walk round museums and see wonderful artefacts in glass cases, we may read about the customs and fashions of other countries. It may all be very interesting—but will it *change* us?

The description of the scent of a rose will not. The scent of a rose may.

*

The *Upanishads*, the *Bhagavad-Gita* and other scriptures contain the *Knowledge* of the Vedas.

But the *Knowledge* is only half the story.

There is also the *Being*.

*

It is our "Being" that first sends us off—searching for Knowledge.

Why should certain people seek Truth (whatever that may mean) while others are perfectly content to live day by day in what the Vedanta calls "illusion"?

NOW we must begin to understand that the Vedas are to do with *work*; work on the self. It is a twofold work.

WORK ON KNOWLEDGE and WORK ON BEING.

The one constantly contributes to the other. As our Knowledge extends (if one can use such an inadequate phrase) so also our Being expands.

Similarly, as our Being thus expands, our capacity to *understand* Truth (to stand under Truth) through Knowledge also expands.

Perhaps "expands" does seem a strange word—but it is all to do with *space*; the creating of *space* within mind and within heart for the Knowledge of Mind and the Being of Love.

*

How can this be accomplished?

The disciple learnt by heart the songs of the Vedas. He repeated them over and over again. He repeated them so often that the *sound* of them became part of him. The Knowledge that the sound "does" (means) became him. He was one with the sound. Thus Work on Knowledge begins.

Meanwhile Work on Being was also taking place.

The exercises that we have already introduced are the beginning.

They are attempts to still the mind; to stop the busy chasing of Manas, and the vague and confused reflecting of Buddhi.

*

Throughout the Sanskrit records of the Vedanta constant emphasis is placed upon the disciple *listening* to the words of the wise (remember that *Upanishad* means literally "at the feet of").

But there is an equal emphasis placed upon *Meditation*.

*

Meditation is by no means a familiar nor widespread practice for people in the "western" world. (Although in recent years there has been a growing interest in the subject as more and more "gurus" have come from the East bearing their gift of meditation, with its promise of all manner of benefit for the diligent student). Indeed, in an English dictionary we find *meditate* defined as:

"Plan mentally, design; exercise the mind in (especially religious) contemplation."

Yet the exercises that we have done so far may perhaps have shown us that, firstly, the mind requires no encouragement to "plan"—to be busy doing; and, secondly, that the mind requires no "exercise"! Quite the reverse!

Meditation is to do with stilling the mind.

Once mind is still, then a technique of meditation may connect the disciple with "the centre of his Being", and what that means—we can only each of us discover for ourselves.

Once again the writers are in difficulty.

You cannot describe meditation—any more than you can describe breathing. It is simply a technique, a means to an end, in precisely the same way that breathing is a technique, and a means to an end—keeping the body alive!

*

If you want to meditate you will have to be guided—and a book cannot guide you personally: a book can only suggest that it might be worthwhile to acquire some technique and guidance.

However, if you want to meditate, and if you follow the exercises that we have already suggested—follow then diligently and regularly—then you may discover the beginning of your very own, simple, personal form of meditation.

For, in the end, only *you* can observe and judge what is happening to you.

Let us be very clear about this:

Meditation—whatever the form—is a technique. It is an exercise to be *used*: specifically devised for Work on Being. It is never an end in itself.

Meditation could be likened to a knife. You can have a sharp knife, you can have a blunt knife. One knife is better for one job, one for another. The knife is only worth what it can do—if it doesn't cut, it is useless: throw it away, and get another one.

With meditation a fine line can be cut right through the illusions in mind, deeper and deeper it can travel—to the very heart of Being. The more often the technique is practised the more sure the line becomes. It is a lifetime's work. But you will not become "top of the form" in meditation. Never. On those very days when it seems that mind will not be stilled—when Manas chases after one thought and then another—when your period of meditation has been nothing but thinking and thinking and thinking, round and round in ever increasing circles . . . do not despair! Do not even judge! It is sufficient that you sat quietly and tried to hear the *sound* of the Self calling from within.

The trying is all; the attempting is all. What more can we ever do?

*

"*The wise, meditating on God, concentrating their thought, discovering in the mouth of the cavern, deeper in the cavern, that Self, that ancient Self, difficult to imagine, more difficult to understand, pass beyond joy and sorrow.*

"*The man that, hearing from the Teacher and comprehending, distinguishes nature from the Self, goes to the source; that man attains joy, lives for ever in that joy . . .*"

(*Katha-Upanishad*)

*

Here is the double-edged sword of the Vedas.

Work on Being and Work on Knowledge.

To have one without the other is to stay bound to the cycle of birth and death.

All knowledge—and you will *think* you "know".

Only the ignorant believe that they know—they claim the knowing as "their own". The wise seek only for union with the Self.

All being—and you will *think* you are "pure".

Only the ignorant believe that they are pure—they claim the "pureness" as "their own". The wise seek only for union with the Self.

The Self Knows. The Self is Pure.

*

Thus *Work on Knowledge* and *Work on Being* are essential to the quest. For if both are diligently undertaken, the aspirant will be filled with well-being. This is represented in the Vedantic tradition by the symbol of the "clockwise" *swastika*, a word derived from the Sanskrit words *su* ("well"), and *asti* ("it is"), i.e., "it is well". (Chosen as an emblem in more recent times, but in anti-clockwise direction by Nazi Germany. This anti-clockwise direction is found in eastern culture as the symbol of Kali, the destroyer).

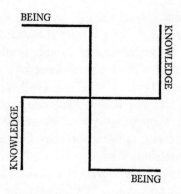

And so, by now there will surely have been readers who will have turned away and said within themselves, "This is much too difficult for me. I do not understand what it is all about," or "I do not see what all this has to do with Hinduism, or any other religion". In so many words, there will be those who will have dismissed the book as being irrelevant to whatever it was they were expecting or hoping to find when they began to read.

We have to recognize that there are different types of people and the various types have different approaches to understanding and require the sustenance of different kinds of "food". Whatever it is that a person desires when being drawn to read a book, the content may well not provide for the nature of that desire, any more than the writer can guarantee that the written word will be conveying exactly what it was that he meant to say.

On the other hand, there will be those to whom the preceding pages have "spoken". They will perhaps have been stirred and they will have found themselves in sympathy with the gist of what the authors are attempting to convey of their own experience of the human state—and how it develops and arrives at a certain condition. And further, that having reached this condition, there is felt the need for help.

For, we may surmise, the response provoked by the ideas expressed in these pages may well be leaving many questions in their wake.

How can we anticipate what those questions may be?

Of course we cannot anticipate the many forms of questions that may have been provoked. This is why the Vedic tradition places such emphasis on the verbal teacher-disciple relationship (and why education of any kind without the presence of a teacher has considerable limitation.) There will be individual response expressed in individual manner; and it is in exploration of that immediate response that the real opportunity for understanding occurs. A real question left unattended is an opportunity lost, and the cause of discomforting mental frustration.

In the ideal situation, the "teacher" and the "disciple" together verbally explore the provocation and the response and see where it leads. (And by "teacher", in the Vedic tradition of spiritual development, we do not necessarily imply one who, knowing all the answers, tries to tell the disciple what he should know. The emphasis is always that the teacher is the more liberated one who may be able to help the other to see the illusion in his or her own believing and thinking so that he or she may become self-liberated. The disciple must see the untruth for himself; realize the Truth for himself. And in the relationship, the disciple frequently "teaches" the teacher at the same time!).

This may well provoke the frustrated response, "Then what is the point of reading such a book as this? How can I possibly participate in such a process if I am here, alone, just reading these words? What do I do now?"

We will pursue this valid response in a moment—after mentioning the possibility of a third category of reader.

This might be the person who understands very clearly what is being said so that these pages are not suggesting anything "new" to him. He or she already inwardly recognizes (re-knows) it within so that what is being said is a confirmation. For such a person the "sound" of this book will be harmonious.

*

But to return to what might be helpful to say to someone to whom the ideas appeal and who sympathizes with the gist of what we have been proposing and who is now stirred to ask probing questions.

Perhaps all that we can say is that once "awakened" to the possibilities inherent in the essential Hindu philosophy, then this book will have done all it can do. It is then up to the awakened one to begin to explore on his or her own account—to be on the look-out for the opportunity to discover further.

How can this be done?

There seem to be two possibilities, neither of them necessarily simple nor easy to pursue.

The first is to seek out others of "like-mind". It may from time to time be one other person or a group of others wishing to discuss and explore such ideas and teachings. Such people may belong to secular societies or religious institutions specifically dedicated to the Vedic tradition (Hindu, Buddhist, etc.) or possibly friends or acquaintances of catholic disposition who are attracted to understanding religion in any form. For as the Vedic tradition asserts (and as the contemporary Hindu with traditional tolerance and magnanimity would corroborate) the crux of the matter is not what religious form a man may adopt but whether in doing so he understands the meaning of being religious and living a religious life. In so many ways, the tradition says that "there are many paths to the top of a mountain. Once at the top it does not matter how you got there."

What is important in joining with another or others in the exploration is the co-operative endeavour, for the understanding arises out of exchange, where there is alternately both giving and taking. It is as if you have to see your own nature reflected back from "the other".

The second possibility is to work on yourself in the sense of observing as often as you remember what is going on in your mind—and realizing what there is in your thinking, believing and assuming that is unreasonable and without sensible foundation. It is useful to look at the beliefs—layer upon layer of them—which have been absorbed through learning and conditioning and which, once the possibility has been admitted, can be seen never to have been contentedly believed. This opens the possibility of giving them up—which should be a relief! (This is not an invitation to become irresponsible; rather it is one to remove that which is preventing your being *naturally* responsible or responsive.)

Such self-observation can be greatly encouraged by reading the scriptures and the many commentaries, ancient and modern, which have been written over the centuries by the "masters".

\*

But, that being said, one of the many questions-cum-objections that we could anticipate would be something along these lines, "But even if I go along with all this, even if I agree with all that you have said, even if I accept that what you have been saying is obvious and reasonable . . . I am so involved in so many things. I do not have time to read scriptures, to have discussions, to think about it all. I forget to watch myself. How can I remember if I am continually forgetting? I forget to remember . . . it is a vicious circle!"

\*

This is where ritual and discipline come into the picture.

Religious traditions have always recognized that a man needs to be put in a situation where he is continually reminded. Whilst he is too "weak" to remember continually for himself, he needs to put himself under a discipline where he can be frequently prompted.

And so all forms of religion introduce an element of discipline and stress the importance of giving precedence, over all other matters, to regular and appropriate practices. For it is recognized that without frequent "putting in mind", the individual will not have the power or persistence to interrupt his or her own devices (unless he or she happens to be one of those rare beings, sometimes called "friends of God", who are able to find their own way without assistance.)

The observance of the disciplines, rituals and practices holds no guarantee. If they are not to be purely repetitive performances blindly carried out, they require the effort of the participant to realize what effect they are having (in much the same way that the doctor's ministrations are rendered next to useless if the patient has no will to get better). There must be trust and willingness to accept instruction and then to carry out that instruction. In other words, they depend for their value on the "longing in the heart for Truth".

What is more, without proper supervision, the disciplines and practices can be turned to self-improvement, self-aggrandizement and escape from one self-delusion into another. There can easily be temptation to divert from the real purpose—Self-Knowledge or Self-Realization.

There must then be honest work and effort on the part of the aspirant. Just attending the "temple", performing the rituals, and mouthing the prayers or chants in the company of others may be comforting and reassuring; but such participation is not really the point. There has to be active longing for Truth.

Of course, no one can will himself or anyone else to have such longing. Either it is there or it is not.

If it is there, it may be weak and spasmodic or strong and persistent. Why should it vary from one to another? Because, the Vedic tradition would say, it depends on "past lives" and how they have been lived. It depends on karma—the effect of past deeds. "Young souls" are too fascinated by the world to be bothered with "longing for Truth"; "old souls" tire easily of the world's blandishments and wish to find their way back to the "cause" or Truth of themselves. (And "young" and "old" here has nothing to do with the age of the present body.)

There is enormous variation in the degrees to which "souls" are *involving* themselves in the world or are in the process of *evolving* themselves out of it.

And seen in true perspective, there can be no judgement, pride or condemnation one of another, no matter where each happens to stand at the moment. (Anymore than it would be appropriate for a butterfly to belittle a caterpillar or for a caterpillar to envy a butterfly.) For sooner or later, the scriptures assure us, all "souls" go through the process of involution and evolution. Different "souls" are at different stages . . . and that is how it is. No question of it being otherwise.

This perspective, inherent in the Vedic knowledge, again invests Hinduism with its reputation for tolerance and flexibility (and its attitude towards death, which carries nothing like the same connotation of finality that it does in other traditions). The Hindu does not try to persuade or convert and, historically, Hinduism shows little sign of proselytism. If for the time being someone calls himself a Hindu, a Christian, a Muslim, a Jew or an atheist . . . so be it. The label has nothing to do with where a person is on the path of evolution; it is only what he has chosen to call himself for the time being.

*

But to return to practices associated with Hinduism.

On the face of it, there can be found all the performances and trappings that emerge at a certain point in the evolution of any religion, when it starts to become institutionalized.

In the Hindu calendar there are many official occasions for ritual worship both in the temple and in the home.

The public sacred places, ranging from grand temples to roadside shrines, are respected as "dwelling places of the gods"—not, we should repeat, as separate "entities" but as particular manifestations of the Ultimate Supreme Being, called Brahman. And according to the wealth and importance of the particular shrine, so it will be well attended, richly furnished and looked after by a greater or lesser number of temple-priests. (Their responsibility is to the temple or shrine—not to the people who come from time to time to pay homage there.)

The gods and goddesses—Vishnu and his consort, Lakshmi; Brahma with Sarasvati; Shiva with his various consorts, Sati, Parvati, Durga and Kali; Ganesa, Krishna, and so on—all have their symbolic images through which are represented the powers, qualities and characteristics of the One Absolute Reality, Brahman.

The individual worshipper, according to his or her preferences, may approach the Absolute Being, through any of the forms taken by that Being. Hence the apparent polytheism—which, fundamentally, is nothing of the kind.

*

The Indian mythology concerning the cause, creation and organization of the universe is vast. And we cannot in this book even begin to explore its richness and complexity, nor the extraordinary parallels and similarities that it has with, say, Babylonian or Jewish/Christian mythology.

But we may touch briefly on one or two principles which may help to demonstrate that the oldest traditions have common foundation.

The Supreme Being—the "One God"—is said to be "unknowable" because "It" cannot be conceived of by the human mind. (If the One was "knowable", there would be two—the knower and the known—man *and* God, which is total contradiction of God's Omnipotence and Omniscience). In order that the Supreme Being may be acknowledged by the human mind, "It" has to divide and manifest Itself as creation.

And so, in the myth, this Supreme Being, Brahman, is said to desire to create and in so doing divides Itself into a triad of powers or forces called Brahma—the Creator, Vishnu—the Preserver and Shiva—the Dissolver or Destroyer.

This trinity is in continuous interplay whilst there is manifest creation. And we experience and see them as the threefold force in operation in any event.

In Brahma we see all endeavour to create new form; in Vishnu we see all endeavour to preserve continuity of that form; and in Shiva we see that inevitably in creating new form there has to be the complementary dissolution or destruction of old forms, because, in the one sum total of everything existing, nothing can be added and nothing subtracted. Creation of something always means destruction of something else and *vice versa*. You cannot take without there being giving at the same time. Which is why Shiva, the Destroyer, is not necessarily "negative", and is sometimes said to be "creative". If I "destroy" an apple by eating it, simultaneously I am "creating" food for myself. Meanwhile, "in between" creation and destruction is the third force, Vishnu, arbitrating or conditioning the continuity, preservation or maintenance of balance.

In other words, in modern scientific terms, we could say that we are describing the laws of energy exchange. (And thus, for modern man, scientific facts are his "gods". It is only a case of changing labels).

Each member of the trinity, in its relationship with the other two in a particular context, is sometimes the active factor, sometimes the passive and sometimes the conditioning factor.

And because it is not possible to be two factors simultaneously, each god has changing function.

For example, the active–passive alternation is represented by male–female so that each god has its consort goddess or goddesses. (And it is important to stress again that the god and goddess are not essentially seen as two *separate* entities; they are the twofold function of the *same* power.)

Brahma's female aspect, Sarasvati, is the "goddess of the arts and sciences". Vishnu's consort, Lakshmi, is the "goddess of wealth and prosperity". Shiva's female aspect, Shakti, is subtle and complex and has to be represented by several images because of the various ways in which sexual power can manifest and be understood. Fundamentally, it is to do with survival in its broadest and profoundest sense. In its benign aspects, Sati and Parvati, it can mean: loving, the dissolving of differences, sacrifice to new birth and life, both physical and spiritual. In its active aspects, Durga and Kali, as the agents of cleansing, purifying and elimination of waste, it can mean: anger, destruction of the useless, rectifying punishment, the killing of the enemies of truth, the annihilation of evil, transformation or dissolution by death itself.

\*

In this brief introduction to the principal gods and goddesses, we may catch a glimpse of the Hindu cosmology—a wide-ranging, all-embracing representation of man's comprehension of the universe and the powers and laws that govern all things, their processes and relationships—which, of course, includes all aspects of man's role in creation and dissolution.

To what extent it has been, and is now, understood, we cannot judge, but at least we may not now so readily dismiss the Hindu religious form as just a superstitious worship of idols.

*

So what else ought we to mention of the practices in Hinduism?

The paying of homage to the gods and goddesses—which may, as in any other religion, degenerate into idol-worship born of selfish desire and fear—represents man's acknowledgement of the powers to which he is subject.

And although there is much public ceremony associated with celebrating and paying homage to these god and goddess powers, it is really predominantly in his own home that the Hindu pursues his religious aspiration, according to his or her own nature and preference. A room or corner of the house will be the focus for family and private worship. And inevitably therefore, religious practice is part and parcel of domestic life, punctuating the day from dawn to dusk, and is not something that he has to go out to find at set times according to when services are being held at public places of worship, supervised and conducted by "officials".

Although he may ask for help or advice from a priest (*brahmin*)—and invite his participation in the important customs and rituals associated with birth, marriage and death—and may listen to the expounding of a learned man (*pandit*), he would recognize that at heart the Hindu dispensation throws the responsibility onto the individual to find his own way to Brahman, the Ultimate Reality. He may rely on pure devotion (*bhakti*) or may aspire also through knowledge (*veda*) and understanding for which purpose he may seek out a spiritual teacher (*guru* or *acharya*) who will give him personal instructions and discipline.

135

In putting himself under a spiritual teacher, the aspirant accepts that he needs help in overcoming the inertia, ignorance and illusion in himself—that which is preventing his realization of Reality.

His goal is *yoga* which means "union". His longing is to be united with Brahman. And it is not that "he", as a separate entity, "goes to" Brahman, as a second "entity"—one joining another One. It is more that through cleansing, purification, the emerging from ignorance, the dissolving of illusion, the surrendering of self-concern—however such sacrifice may be termed—"he" dissolves in the Reality and It becomes manifest in him—for as long as he remains incarnate. This is liberation (*moksha*). And, beyond that, the final Yoga or Union at death—which is a culmination to be welcomed, not dreaded.

Ultimately, Atman (the Self) is liberated from Maya (Illusion) and becomes One with Brahman (Reality), "as the drop of dew eventually merges with the sea".

*

And here we ought to make a slight diversion to help clarify the character of Hindu viewpoint.

The Vedic tradition recognizes two important factors.

Firstly that the human life has phases. That may seem obvious but it is surprising how the implications of it become blurred in modern society's estimation of what a man or woman really needs at different times in life. For the atheist or materialist it does not matter, for the growth, maintenance and decline of the physical and mental capacities are inevitable and he can do what he likes between birth and death. But the implications for the religious or spiritual life of the aspirant are significant. Particular instructions, disciplines and practices may be appropriate at one stage but may not be so at another.

Basically the four divisions of a life are described as "studying" (which is learning to take a place in society), "house-holding" (which is playing an adult role in the well-being, commerce and survival of society), "retiring" (which is withdrawing from active participation so that "the lessons of life" may be "digested"—and, if required, perhaps making "wisdom" available for the benefit of society)—and, fourthly, "seclusion" (which means complete withdrawal from the affairs and attachments of society for the resolution of "this" life and contemplation of the "after-life").

Of course, we have "echoes" of these phases in contemporary society and the first three are common enough in secular life. But the fourth is not evident in the materialist or atheist.

Another way of describing the above would be that in the first phase, we learn; in the second, we relate and apply that learning to experience; in the third, we distil wisdom out of the first two; and, in the fourth, we resolve all three into understanding.

*

And the second important factor to take into account is that the Vedic tradition acknowledges the different constitutions of people (due to the varying permutations in them of the basic elements that give the quality, content and form of the individual). Again this may seem obvious but, in its estimation of society's needs, does not government and administration repeatedly treat individuals as if they are all the same? Do we not tend to find this tendency in education, medicine and other social services?

For the individual to be able to fulfil himself or herself, it ought to be understood what the person's capacities and talents are, ideally in advance of the education process. Frequently in modern society it is left to haphazard circumstance or the limited experience of the growing individual to discover the potential. And, alas, that potential is often either discovered too late or not at all and a person can easily spend his or her life in an inappropriate role.

Not only did the Vedic tradition apparently acknowledge this individual potential but it was sufficiently wise to be able to recognize the signs of its character at a very early age. The wise ones of their societies could discern a disposition or a talent in a child accurately enough to ensure that his or her education was appropriate to the fulfilment of that potential. And, again, this potential would only incidentally have been in terms of appropriate work occupation; essentially the work that a person performed would be of a kind most conducive to spiritual development. Work and the religious life were inextricably inter-dependent.

And here again there were four basic categories—the "labourer" (*shudra*), the "tradesman-farmer-craftsman" (*vaishya*), the "warrior-leader" (*kshatriya*) and the "teacher-priest" (*brahmin*). We could say that these again are "labels" which suggest the dominant elements in different kinds of people—say "earth", "water", "fire" and "air". There was ideally no implication of superiority or inferiority in these divisions; all occupations would be performed in service to Brahman and each person's capacity for "liberation" was equal through his or her own particular form of service to the community.

There were also much subtler sub-divisions of these categories to be identified, with the aid for example of the science of astrology (which has virtually nothing to do, in terms of intelligence and application, with what is popularly called "astrology" today).

We cannot further divert here in detail so let it suffice for us to suggest that such present-day phenomena as the Hindu caste system and prediction-of-my-worldly-future astrology are the debased and shadowy vestiges of what was once an intelligent assessment of the roles and circumstances best suited for an individual's fulfilment in life.

\*

The point of this diversion into the Vedic acknowledgement of "types" is that, in parallel, it was understood that different individuals were suited to different forms of religious instruction and discipline.

Basically, these could be predominantly through the body (physical, ascetic disciplines), through the heart and emotions (devotional service) and through the head (discrimination and philosophy).

Thus the practice of Yoga is divided into categories—*hatha-yoga, karma-yoga, jnana-yoga* and so on.

What the West has recently adopted and happily called "yoga" tends to be just a section of the practice of *hatha-yoga* (bodily postures, exercises, especially breathing exercises). This may well be beneficial in terms of physical and emotional health, but it is a pale shadow of the real intent—spiritual fulfilment through Union with Ultimate Reality via "mastery" of the body and its energies.

At the same time, we must add, there are undoubtedly teachers who do understand the full measure of Yoga (and it may well be that they would not necessarily call it by that name because "union with the divine" is the common and ultimate goal of all religions.)

By whatever name and at whatever level they are practised, the methods and disciplines of Yoga are all "steps on the ladder" to Reality.

\*

Once again, the value of such disciplines is that the aspirant *puts himself* under them and they become regular "re-minders". Because, to return to our earlier terminology, they serve to help the aspirant remember the presence of the Self, the real "I" manifesting in the being as "I am".

Perhaps we can begin to see therefore that all the disciplines are essentially disciplines of the mind. Whether it be physical discipline, or emotional, or intellectual—all demand "strength" of mind.

The mind, one way or another, comes to understand by whose Will "it is done".

\*

Ever beholding that supreme Self everywhere, resting thy thought in the secondless Self, let the time pass for thee, mighty-minded, in the experience of the bliss of the Self.

Conceiving separateness in that partless Self of illumination, which is without separateness, is like building dwellings in the air; therefore, gaining supreme serenity through the Self which is ever secondless joy, rejoice in silence.

The Soul's supreme tranquility, brooding in silence, dissolves the unsubstantial buildings of the mind; from this, through the supreme Self, which is the Eternal, straightway comes joy in undivided bliss.

There is no more excellent source of joy than silence free from all mind-images, for him who has discerned the true being of the Self, drinking in the essence of the joy of the Self.

(*Vivekachudamani*)

WEARIED by too much thinking in the busy mind of your busier world    *now*    turn back, 180 degree turn, look deep into yourself. Thoughts come and go, let them go; pay them no heed; do not resist them coming—why should they not? But do not entertain them either—why should you? Go to that deepest point, reach for it, search for it; the deepest point within the heart of you; the deepest ...................................................

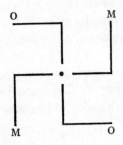

...........................................the deepest; from deep within the heart of you, return, gradually, little by little. Reach for the world again, search for it. Thoughts are there, coming and going. They have every right to be there—discriminate, observe, experience    *now*    turn out, 180 degrees turn, meet the world once more—enjoy, being REFRESHED

*

By whose Will is the universe created?

By whose Will are we born into this universe?

By whose Will do we come to play our roles in the universe—and to what purpose do we play those roles?

*

These are the questions that we may presume man has always asked, just as we are asking them now.

How are we able to ask them?

Because we are here and because we *know* we are here.

By the strange phenomenon that we call "consciousness", apparently peculiar to the human being amongst all creatures, we have the capacity to be aware of our existence.

And because of that capacity to be "self-conscious", we are able to contemplate the mystery of our existence and our relationship with the universe.

It is on this simple experience that every religion and every philosophy depends. They are all attempts to explain and cope with the implications of man's ability to be *aware* that he *is*.

*

From time to time, when we remember or are reminded, we may wake up to the experience of our simply "being".

I am.

What is more, "I *know* I am".

In passing time I may become many things, saying that "I am this" or "I am that". In believing thus, the "being aware of myself" is lost in all the implications of the belief. "I am" becomes lost, as it were, in the illusion or dream of what "I think I am".

From there on, it is all *bound* to happen to "me".

*

The Vedic tradition speaks of levels of consciousness and we may now describe a number of them:

| | |
|---|---|
| "deep sleep" | — absence of Self-consciousness. |
| "dream sleep" | — sufficient consciousness to illuminate the discursive activity of uncontrolled mind; still no Self-consciousness. |
| "waking sleep" | — consciousness of the world and of the activity in it. Nevertheless, "lost" in it and still no Self-consciousness. |
| "awake" | — consciousness or awareness of "being", "I know I am", Self-consciousness. |
| "higher states of consciousness" | — "withdrawal" to the real "I", remembering "God", leading to "knowing God", Self-realization. |

*

What can be understood by "withdrawal to the I" in what we have called "higher states of consciousness"?

We have touched on it in a number of ways in this book (and in all the other books in this series). In terms of the "return journey" we could say that having, without conscious choice, come into the world and taken our places in it, at a certain point we may *choose consciously* to work our way out of it again. In doing so we complete within the one lifetime a natural cycle of creation, preservation and dissolution. In terms of the labyrinth or maze, we could say that, having by trial and error learned to find our way through it, the really important complement is to remember consciously the way back again. In terms of religion we could say that we have fallen into fascination with the world and into self-concern; in so doing we have ignored "God" and our salvation depends on remembering and surrendering to "Him" through a process of "renouncing the world and the flesh". In terms of Vedic-cum-Hindu philosophy, we could say that it means that, having through arbitrary learning and conditioning become bound by illusory beliefs, we must through contemplation and reason come to understand the Ultimate Reality or the Truth.

In whatever terms we express it, it seems that a cycle must complete itself. The "spirit" which came into us and enlivened us with the first breath and which then dwells within us to give continuing life is forgotten by mind as it dreams and sleeps. Mind may then remember and become aware of its presence. Having acknowledged its presence, the mind, through a process of "surrendering", may *consciously* allow the "spirit" to be liberated and to return to the source.

Each of us is created, maintained and then either "destroyed" or "dissolved". In one aspect, Shiva must destroy that which has passed its usefulness; thus we die into the unconsciousness of death. In its other aspect, Shiva acts as "midwife to the soul" which is "born again" out of the "flesh"; thus we die to the world and "rise" consciously into "eternal life".

\*

*"He who knows that the senses belong not to Spirit, but to the elements, that they are born and die, grieves no more.*

*"Mind is above sense, intellect above mind, nature above intellect, the unmanifest above nature.*

*"Above the unmanifest is God, unconditioned, filling all things. He who finds Him enters immortal life, becomes free.*

*"No eye can see Him, nor has He a face that can be seen, yet through meditation and through discipline He can be found in the heart. He that finds Him enters immortal life . . ."*

(*Katha–Upanishad*)

\*

This "withdrawal" is not to suggest that we should "renounce the world" in the sense of spurning it and having nothing to do with it (although certain monastic and hermetic disciplines do take it almost that literally). On the contrary, the Vedas would seem to advocate that whilst we are here we should *"hope for a hundred years of life doing your duty"*.

The Hindu speaks of four goals in life. The first is to find the way of righteousness in which one's own duty (*dharma*) is thoroughly understood; the second is to discover the key to "well-being" (*artha*); the third is to be able to live in joy (*kama*); and, finally, the

144

fourth is to achieve liberation (*moksha*)—which is the withdrawal aspect. It may seem paradoxical, but enjoyment, it is suggested, is not incompatible with withdrawal; on the contrary, withdrawal from attachment and dependence on "things" permits the freedom of natural enjoyment. It is a case of enjoyment *in* the world and not *of* the world.

\*

*It is better to do your own duty, however imperfectly, than to assume the duties of another person, however successfully. Prefer to die doing your own duty: the duty of another will bring you into great spiritual danger.*
(*Bhagavad-Gita*)

\*

One of the keys to enjoyment is what the Vedic tradition might describe as being free of the belief in success and failure.

We tend to be so drawn in and obsessed, or "possessed", by the possible outcome or result of our endeavour that we forget to enjoy the endeavour itself. We become so concerned that our efforts should result in future success that we often fail to watch, regulate and take pleasure in the present moment.

Yet, if we pause to consider, exactly what do we expect our success to provide in lasting and real terms?

How well do we really understand the nature of our supposed success?

Do we take into account how transitory, ephemeral, subjective and relative success and failure are, in the world's terms?

Again, this must not be to suggest that there should be no attempt to "succeed" in our endeavour. It is not an invitation to apathy and idleness—far from it. The exhortation is to do whatever task presents itself to the best of one's capabilities, with all possible care and attention and with all possible enjoyment. How well a task is done can be so hampered by worrying about the result and being prejudiced as to what the result should be. Thus the emphasis is on letting the result take care of itself because we can never guarantee it; we do not have the power to manipulate all the factors which would account the result successful; and in any case there is no such thing as absolute success in the eyes of the world.

\*

*You have the right to work, but for the work's sake only. You have no right to the fruits of work. Desire for the fruits of work must never be your motive in working. Never give way to laziness, either.*

*Perform every action with your heart fixed on the Supreme Lord. Renounce attachment to the fruits. Be even-tempered in success and failure; for it is this evenness of temper which is meant by yoga.*

*Work done with anxiety about results is far inferior to work done without such anxiety, in the calm of self-surrender. Seek refuge in the knowledge of Brahman. They who work selfishly for results are miserable.*

*In the calm of self-surrender you can free yourself from the bondage of virtue and vice during this very life. Devote yourself, therefore, to reaching union with Brahman. To unite the heart with Brahman and then to act: that is the secret of non-attached work. In the calm of self-surrender, the seers renounce the fruits of their actions, and so reach enlightenment. Then they are free from the bondage of rebirth, and pass to that state which is beyond all evil.*

*(Bhagavad-Gita)*

\*

Performing one's *own* duty without *worrying* about success or failure of the result is one of the main themes related to the first three goals mentioned above.

But how about the fourth, "liberation"?

Liberation, we have already suggested, is to do with freedom from illusory belief (and, in this sense, not worrying about results is a liberation) and is thus connected with withdrawal from what is realized as being false—not what we judge to be false *in the world* but what we realize to be false *in ourselves*. There is absolutely no benefit to be gained in blaming our misfortunes on anyone else.

However, as has been said, it is very difficult in the momentum of the daily round to remember—to "create" space by listening, to "stand back" and keep things in perspective.

146

And this is perhaps why, somewhere back in the Vedic history, there emerged the practice of what we have called "meditation" (and in other religions the practice of "prayer").

*

Although we have already said that what meditation *is* each person must discover for himself or herself, there are perhaps a few things that can be said *about* it.

The word itself implies "being in the middle" or perhaps "being the medium for something".

It is not unlike the English word "mediate" as defined in the dictionary: "Form connecting link between; intervene (between two persons) for purpose of reconciling them; be the medium of bringing about (result) or conveying (gift etc.)."

Meditation carries a suggestion of a two-way responsibility of the mind, or that it is a state of mind which allows a two-way process to take place

In its "outwards" direction it suggests passivity:

pausing between activities and tasks,

remembering,

quietening the mind ("stilling Manas")

contemplating and reflecting ("clearing or cleaning Buddhi")

listening,

creating "space" in the mind through surrendering self-concern,

becoming the intermediary, the mediator, between the Supreme Being and the World.

surrendering self-will to "higher" Will,

being naturally responsive to need,

wondering,

being full of joy, gratitude, praise, bliss,

giving full attention, to the All as One.

......

In its "inwards" direction, it suggests active withdrawal:

creating "inner" space,

listening "inwardly" to the "silence",

sacrificing self-will,

longing for Union with the Divine,
all desire and movement ceasing,
no sensation, no concept, no thought,
"touching eternity",
the bliss-consciousness of the All as No-thing,
dissolution

......

Beyond "inwards" and "outwards" is the realization of the One that is All and No-thing, Mind being the Space in which Realization takes Place.

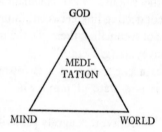

In meditation, "God breathes out" in creating, Realizes Himself, and "breathes in" dissolving the creation.

*

*As he sits there, he is to hold the senses and the imagination in check, and keep the mind concentrated upon its object. If he practises meditation in this manner, his heart will become pure.*

*His posture will be motionless, with the body, head and neck held erect, and the vision indrawn, as if gazing at the tip of the nose. He must not look about him.*

> *So, with his heart serene and fearless,*
> *Firm in the vow of renunciation,*
> *Holding the mind from its restless roaming,*
> *Now let him struggle to reach my oneness,*
> *Ever-absorbed, his eyes on me always,*
> *His prize, his purpose.*
>
> *(Bhagavad-Gita)*

148

"God breathes out . . . "
And in so doing the Word is spoken . . . and the All is formed.
Brahman means "Word".
The sound of the Word forms All Things.
And Man listens and hears the Word of All Things.

LISTEN TO THE SILENCE
ALL THINGS SOUND IN THE SILENCE
BRAHMAN IS THE SILENCE BEYOND ALL SOUND

*

What Word?
What is this "Word" that forms All Things—that sounds in the silence?
The Vedas describes the word as three-fold and it is sometimes written:

OM

although to represent its three aspects it is also written as AUM.

Pronounced correctly (almost like "home" without the "h"), the form of the sound of the word is said to be the purest syllable. When intoned it travels a complete octave and, in incorporating expression of breath, the use of the throat, the palate and the lips, and including the closed-mouth, nasal sound of the "M", it encompasses all vocal possibilities.

The sound is the matrix from which all other sounds may be developed, with the help of the tongue. And such is its power that it is said to be able to evoke the whole range of human emotion.

In it we can see the Hindu trinity of powers represented—Brahma creates, from the breath of the first vowel "A", with the vocal chords; Vishnu moulds and holds the sound in the containing space of the mouth ("U"); and Shiva cuts off the open sound so that the breath dies in the fading hum of the "M".

At its deepest and most refined—that is to say when it is heard by one who is finely enough "tuned" to receive it—the Word can be "heard", vibrating through the universe.

*Nachiketas asked: "What lies beyond right and wrong, beyond cause and effect, beyond past and future?"*

*Death said: "The word that the Vedas extol, austerities proclaim, sanctities approach—that word is OM.*

*"That word is eternal Spirit, eternal distance; who knows it attains to his desire.*

*"That word is the ultimate foundation. Who finds it is adored among the saints.*

*"The Self knows all, is not born, does not die, is not the effect of any cause; is eternal, self-existent, imperishable, ancient. How can the killing of the body kill Him?*

*"He who thinks that He kills, he who thinks that He is killed, is ignorant. He does not kill, nor is He killed . . . "*

*(Katha-Upanishad)*

*

Beyond that, little remains to be said.

We have attempted to "reach to the stars".

The Vedas ask us to listen and to understand what we hear.

Our written words are puny descriptions and explanations. As we suggested at the beginning, their only function may be to indicate a direction. "I cannot give you experience of the sun," they may say, "but I can tell you where it is shining."

We cannot say that Hinduism is this or that. It is not a religion in the sense of "you" and "me" believing and having faith in "a god". It is religious in that it indicates man's responsibility to acknowledge and realize "higher" Will. It is philosophical in that it indicates the nature of real Knowledge. It is psychological in that it essentially involves study of the mind and how it works.

But beyond all that description and explanation, it is pointing to the need of man to observe his experience—to realize through that experience the purpose of the "soul's journey" into and out of creation.

In which process the Self is realized.

*

*"The Self is lesser than the least, greater than the greatest. He lives in all hearts. When senses are at rest, free from desire, man finds Him and mounts beyond sorrow.*

*"Though sitting, He travels; though sleeping is everywhere. Who but I Death can understand that God is beyond joy and sorrow.*

*"Who knows the Self, bodiless among the embodied, unchanging among the changing, prevalent everywhere, goes beyond sorrow.*

*"The Self is not known through discourse, splitting of hairs, learning however great; He comes to the man He loves; takes that man's body for His own . . .*

(Katha-Upanishad)

*

No one can be persuaded to follow a particular direction for long if it is not natural to his nature.

I may be compelled by someone to read a book—but, if I am not interested in the words, they will not become a part of me.

Why should I be "interested?" What is this interest?

Perhaps each is called to his own path.

It all depends on what is happening as your eyes scan along this line of words . . . *now* . . .

*

No one can be persuaded to meditate, if they do not want to do so.

You can be made to sit down and adopt a suitable posture. You may control your body movement and you may set your face in what you assume to be a suitable "meditating expression".

You may, in short, fool all those who are looking *at* you that you are meditating.

But only you know what is going on within.

Only *you* can meditate for you.

Or so it seems—until one day the question arises . . .

"Who meditates?"

. . . and another "sheath of illusion" begins to fall.

＊

For in the end (or at the beginning), it all depends upon what each of us wants, upon what we deeply desire.

What is it that *you* desire?

Did you choose that desire?

If not, then perhaps it should be trusted—regardless of what anyone else may tell you.

Trust the desire, and with it begin a journey.

It is a journey that each of us must make in our own way.

We have been born into this world, and, at birth, we have each been given the gift of self-hood, with a body to carry the self and a mind-vehicle to receive "food".

We are set for the journey.

And now the desires rise.

All that we require is that someone should take us and point out to us the direction of our destination.

## EXPERIENCE
## OBSERVATION
## DISCRIMINATION

Now the journey is along a path that each of us must tread for ourSelf.

＊

What is it that *I* desire?

＊

## LISTEN

＊

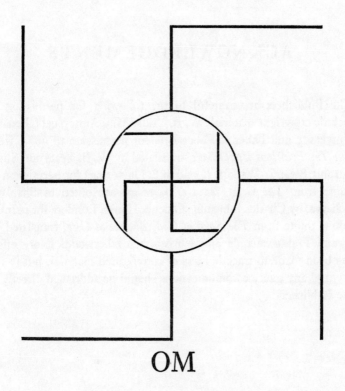

OM

# ACKNOWLEDGEMENTS

The Publishers are grateful to the following for permission to include copyright material: W. B. Yeats, Miss Anne Yeats, Benares University and Faber & Faber Ltd. for permission to quote from *The Ten Principal Upanishads*, translated by W. B. Yeats and Shree Purohit Swami; Watkins (London & Dulverton) for permission to quote from *The Crest Jewel of Wisdom*—attributed to Shankara Acharya, by Charles Johnston; Phoenix House, London, for permission to quote from *The Song of God*, *Bhagavad-Gita*, translated by Swami Prabhavananda and Christopher Isherwood. Every effort has been made to trace holders of copyrighted material, but in the event of any query communications should be addressed directly to the Publishers.